The Law Commission
(LAW COM No 301)

TRUSTEE EXEMPTION CLAUSES

Presented to the Parliament of the United Kingdom by the Secretary of State for Constitutional Affairs and Lord Chancellor by Command of Her Majesty July 2006

Cm 6874   London: The Stationery Office   £16.00

The Law Commission was set up by the Law Commissions Act 1965 for the purpose of promoting the reform of the law.

The Law Commissioners are:

The Honourable Mr Justice Toulson, *Chairman*
Professor Hugh Beale QC, FBA
Mr Stuart Bridge
Dr Jeremy Horder
Mr Kenneth Parker QC

The Chief Executive of the Law Commission is Mr Steve Humphreys.

The Law Commission is located at Conquest House, 37-38 John Street, Theobalds Road, London WC1N 2BQ.

The terms of this report were agreed on 20 June 2006.

The text of this report is available on the Internet at:

http://www.lawcom.gov.uk

THE LAW COMMISSION

TRUSTEE EXEMPTION CLAUSES

CONTENTS

PART 1
INTRODUCTION

1.1 This paper reports on the results of the Law Commission's consultation on trustee exemption clauses and sets out our recommendations. It should be read with reference to Trustee Exemption Clauses, Law Commission Consultation Paper No 171 ("the CP").

1.2 The project has considered clauses which exclude or restrict a trustee's liability for breach of trust, either by expressly excluding liability or by modifying the trustee's powers and duties.

BACKGROUND TO THE PROJECT

1.3 The Law Commission's project on trustee exemption clauses arose out of the passage through Parliament of the Trustee Bill in 2000. The Trustee Act 2000, based on the recommendations of the Law Commission,[1] adopted a permissive approach to modern trusteeship. It conferred wider powers on trustees and controlled their conduct by the introduction of a statutory duty of care.[2]

1.4 During debates in the House of Lords, Lord Goodhart expressed the concern that the proposed measure did nothing to restrict the use of exemption clauses in trust instruments. This, he argued, raised the possibility of beneficiaries being denied adequate protection.[3]

1.5 The Lord Chancellor responded to Lord Goodhart's concerns by undertaking to refer the matter to the Law Commission for thorough examination. The agreed terms of reference were:

> ... to examine the law governing clauses which restrict the liabilities of trustees either by excluding liability for breach of their duties or by limiting the duties to which the trustees are subject.[4]

1.6 The Trust Law Committee ("TLC") had, in June 1999, issued its own consultation paper on trustee exemption clauses.[5] This paper proposed that a trustee remunerated for his services as trustee should be precluded from relying on an exemption clause excluding liability for breach of trust arising from negligence, at least in circumstances where the trustee could not prove that prior independent advice was given to the settlor. The consultation paper stated:

> There is much to be said for trust corporations and professional individuals paid for their services as trustees, (like solicitors, barristers

---

[1] Trustees' Powers and Duties (1999) Law Com No 260; Scot Law Com No 172.

[2] Trustee Act 2000, s 1(1). The duty of care is capable of exclusion or limitation by words in the trust instrument which indicate that the duty is not meant to apply (Trustee Act 2000, sch 1, para 7).

[3] See Hansard (HL), vol 612, col 383.

[4] See CP, para 1.11.

[5] Trust Law Committee, *Consultation Paper: Trustee Exemption Clauses* (June 1999).

and accountants) to accept the price of liability for negligence in acting as a paid trustee and to insure against such risk, with the premiums being reflected in the fees for the services provided.[6]

THE PROJECT

Research

1.7 Before formulating its provisional policy proposals the Law Commission sought to ascertain views on the use of trustee exemption clauses and the likely effect of regulation. The Commission distributed a questionnaire to trusts practitioners with the assistance of the Society of Trust and Estate Practitioners ("STEP"). Building on this preliminary survey the Commission instructed Dr Alison Dunn of the Faculty of Law, University of Newcastle-upon-Tyne to conduct detailed socio-economic research on the use of trustee exemption clauses. The findings of Dr Dunn's research are set out in Part III of the CP.

Consultation process

1.8 The Commission's consultation paper on trustee exemption clauses was published in January 2003. The paper argued that the law governing trustee exemption clauses was in need of reform, made wide-ranging proposals for legislation, and invited responses. The central provisional proposals were as follows:[7]

(1) A professional trustee should not be able to rely on any provision in a trust instrument excluding liability for breach of trust arising from negligence, and clauses purporting to exclude such liability should be of no effect.

(2) In so far as professional trustees may not exclude liability for breach of trust they should not be permitted to claim indemnity from the trust fund.

(3) Duty exclusion or extended powers clauses should not be prohibited. In determining whether professional trustees have been negligent, the court should, however, be able to disapply such clauses where to rely on them would be inconsistent with the overall purposes of the trust and it would be unreasonable in the circumstances for the trustee to be exempted from liability.

(4) All trustees should be given power to make payments out of the trust fund to purchase indemnity insurance to cover their liability for breach of trust.

(5) Any regulation of trustee exemption clauses should be made applicable not only to trusts governed by English law but also to persons carrying on a trust business in England and Wales.

---

[6] Trust Law Committee, *Consultation Paper: Trustee Exemption Clauses* (June 1999) para 7.8. The TLC has not published a report setting out the results of its consultation or containing final recommendations for reform.

[7] See Part V of the CP for a full list of provisional proposals and consultation questions.

(6)   Any implementing legislation should apply to any breaches of trust which occur on or after the date when the legislation comes into force, but should not apply to breaches of trust which precede that date.

1.9   During the consultation period the Commissioner and the team took part in a number of conferences organised by STEP[8] and a seminar sponsored by the Society of Advanced Legal Studies. The Commissioner also took part in a round table meeting in the City organised by the Centre for the Study of Financial Innovation.

1.10   An important feature of the consultation was the decision by the Financial Markets Law Committee ("FMLC") to set up a working party under Lord Browne-Wilkinson in order to provide a formal written response to the CP and more generally to explain the operation of trusts in financial markets. The FMLC's Report[9] had a major impact on the timing of the project. The team agreed to delay the formulation of final policy recommendations until the FMLC working party had reported and in the meantime progressed its project on the classification and apportionment of trust capital and income.[10]

THE RESPONSE TO CONSULTATION

1.11   The Law Commission received a total of 116 written consultation responses from a wide variety of sources, including trust companies, banks, accountants, judges, legal practitioners, academics, charities and industry groups.[11] Consultees varied enormously in their reaction to the CP and expressed a broad range of views on the issues raised. It was impossible to distil a consensus view on many aspects of this difficult topic.

1.12   The main thrust of responses to the CP may, however, be summarised as follows:

(1)   There was a general distaste for the wide and sometimes indiscriminate inclusion of trustee exemption clauses in trust instruments, especially where the settlor is unaware of their existence or meaning.

(2)   Although there was in consequence support for a degree of regulation of trustee exemption clauses, this was balanced by concerns about its implications for settlor autonomy and the appropriate protection of trustees.

---

[8]   In Leeds, Manchester, Birmingham, Bristol, London and Plymouth.

[9]   Financial Markets Law Committee, *Trustee Exemption Clauses Report – Issue 62* (May 2004)

[10] Capital and Income in Trusts: Classification and Apportionment (2004) Law Com Consultation Paper No 175. The FMLC's Report was issued in May 2004 by which time the Law Commission had decided to take its classification and apportionment project to the consultation paper stage. It is only since the publication of that consultation paper that the team has returned to its consideration of trustee exemption clauses.

[11] See Appendix H for a full list of consultees. The Appendix also refers to a number of articles commenting on the CP.

(3)   The CP's proposed scheme of legislative regulation was more popular than the alternatives considered but rejected in the CP.[12]

(4)   There was serious concern about the CP's proposed treatment of duty modification clauses on the grounds that it would give rise to uncertainty as to whether trustees could rely on the apparent terms of the trust.

(5)   The CP's proposed distinction between professional and lay trustees was considered difficult to apply and liable to cause unfairness (especially in relation to professionals acting pro bono).

(6)   The practicability of the CP's proposal that all trustees should have power to purchase indemnity insurance using the trust funds was questioned on the grounds of cost and availability.

(7)   There was widespread concern about the likely adverse impacts of statutory regulation restricting reliance on trustee exemption clauses. Particular reference was made to the likelihood of increased indemnity insurance premiums and the possible unavailability of insurance; a consequential reluctance on the part of trustees to exercise discretionary powers, if at all, expeditiously and without first taking legal advice; a decrease in the flexibility of the management of trust property; an increase in litigation for breach of trust; and a possible reluctance to accept trusteeship.

(8)   Consultees stressed the very wide range of purposes to which trusts are put. Many charged the Commission with proposing reform aimed at protecting the beneficiaries of private family trusts and ignoring the effects on other sorts of trust.

RE-EXAMINATION OF POLICY

1.13   We have conducted a detailed analysis of consultation responses and reassessed the available evidence in the light of consultees' arguments for and against particular models of regulation. We have concluded as follows:

(1)   Although there is instinctive support for reform of some sort, this does not translate into unambiguous support for any particular type of reform. Many consultees accepted the need for reform, but only in so far as it did not extend to them on the grounds that they were not professional or on the basis that it should not apply to the particular sort of trust with which they were involved.

(2)   Reform should not impinge on settlor autonomy unless absolutely necessary.

(3)   Support for reform is strongest where (i) the settlor is unaware of the existence or meaning of the trustee exemption clause; (ii) the exemption clause is intended to lower the standard of care applicable to the trustee rather than to delineate its responsibilities; (iii) the trustee is paid for

---

[12]   See para 5.2 and Appendix A.

acting as trustee; and (iv) the settlor is not acting in the course of business.

(4)   Any regulation should distinguish between "paid" and "unpaid" trustees.

(5)   In some areas of an increasingly challenging trustee market, trustee exemption clauses currently play a significant role. Duty modification clauses are particularly important to the flexibility of trusts. Since in practice duty modification provisions are often intended to exclude liability, it is difficult to separate out regulation of liability exclusion clauses and duty modification clauses effectively.

(6)   There is no clear alternative protection available to trustees. Trustee indemnity insurance is not capable of filling the role.

(7)   There is a significant risk that statutory regulation of reliance on trustee exemption clauses would give rise to significant adverse consequences. These consequences would impact at least as much on trust beneficiaries as they would on trustees.

(8)   The extent of any mischief posed by trustee exemption clauses remains unclear. It is impossible to be certain how widespread the incidence of trustee negligence is in practice and how often exemption clauses are relied on by trustees.

1.14   There are therefore a number of obstacles to statutory intervention of the sort provisionally proposed in the CP.

1.15   Trustee exemption clauses operate within a complex economic system in which the interests of the three principal players (settlor, trustee and beneficiary) are not always coincidental. Consultation responses confirmed the view that in individual cases a trustee exemption clause may lead to an unfair outcome as it is able to deprive a beneficiary of a remedy for loss sustained as a result of a trustee's breach of trust.

1.16   However, responses also made it clear that restricting the use of exemption clauses in the manner provisionally proposed by the CP could have a negative effect on the system as a whole. Exemption clauses operate to control risk and to keep costs down, thereby encouraging a sufficient number of trustees to operate in the market. Although it is not possible to assess precisely what the impact of restricting trustees' reliance on exemption clauses would be, we have concluded that there is a significant risk that any such legislation could lead to adverse consequences more damaging than anticipated by the CP.[13]

1.17   In addition, we remain aware that any statutory prohibition of reliance on trustee exemption clauses would restrict the autonomy of settlors to determine the terms on which they settle assets on trust. This would, in turn, limit the flexibility of the trust and in doing so detract from one of its greatest attractions.

---

[13]   See para 5.12 and following for a discussion of the potential adverse consequences of a legislative restriction on reliance on exemption clauses.

1.18   Finally, we have not overcome the technical difficulties presented by the use of duty modification provisions. We have been unable to frame legislative regulation in a way which would effectively prevent the use of avoidance mechanisms, other than by creating a system with even greater potential adverse impact.[14]

AN ALTERNATIVE APPROACH

1.19   Consultation has shown that there is, among reputable trustees, a strongly-held belief that trustee exemption clauses should not be included in a trust without the full knowledge and consent of the settlor. We consider the current state of affairs in which many settlors appear to be unaware of the existence or the effect of trustee exemption clauses unacceptable. It undermines the argument that settlors may autonomously decide to grant their trustees the protection of exemption. It also challenges the view that exemption clauses operate in a properly functioning market; the asymmetry of information between the trustee and the settlor has the effect of conferring on the former the benefit of a protection not appreciated by the latter.

1.20   We are of the view that trustees should in some way be required to ensure that the settlors are aware of any trustee exemption clauses in their trust deeds. We believe that many in the trust industry would support this view. An important subsidiary question is whether regulation to achieve this objective should be effected by legislation or by some other means.

1.21   We have considered the option, discussed in the CP, of introducing a statutory requirement that trustees must disclose to the settlor any exemption clause on which they wish to be able to rely. We have rejected this approach for the reasons discussed in Part 6.

1.22   We have concluded that a practice-based approach, rather than legislation, is the better means to bring about reform of the conduct of trustees. This Report recommends a rule of practice that:

> Any paid trustee who causes a settlor to include a clause in a trust instrument which has the effect of excluding or limiting liability for negligence must before the creation of the trust take such steps as are reasonable to ensure that the settlor is aware of the meaning and effect of the clause.[15]

1.23   A rule of practice approach would not suffer the defects that we believe would undermine a statutory scheme. It would require regulated persons to adhere to defined good practice. Breach of this rule would not give rise in itself to liability in damages but would render the trustee open to disciplinary measures by the relevant governing body.[16]

---

[14]   See para 5.38 and following for a discussion of the regulation of duty modification provisions.

[15]   See para 6.65. See para 6.41 and following for discussion of the operation of such a rule and guidance about its precise application (including its application to those that draft trusts).

[16]   See para 6.53 and following.

1.24 In our view, this would be a proportionate response to the failure of the trustee to ensure that there was adequate settlor awareness of a trustee exemption clause. Regulation by professional and trust bodies by means of a rule of practice would, we believe, be the most appropriate and effective means of influencing and informing trustees so as to secure the proper disclosure of exemption clauses.

1.25 During our consultation we have become aware of a number of regulatory and professional bodies who would be prepared to introduce a rule of good practice into their own professional codes of conduct. The England and Wales region of STEP is the first organisation to finalise such a rule.[17] We refer to our discussions with STEP and with other organisations in Part 6.

1.26 Efforts should be made to promote the application of our recommended rule of practice as widely as possible across the trust industry. We encourage relevant regulatory and professional bodies to adopt a version of the rule appropriate to the particular circumstances of their membership, and to enforce such regulation in accordance with their existing codes of conduct.

1.27 We anticipate that the successful adoption of the rule across the trust industry will significantly ameliorate the problems associated with trustee exemption clauses. It will ensure that such provisions represent a proper and fully informed expression of the terms on which settlors are willing to dispose of their property on trust.

STRUCTURE OF THIS REPORT

1.28 This Report explains how we have arrived at our recommendations.

1.29 In Part 2, we give a brief summary of the current law as it applies to trustee exemption clauses. In Part 3, we consider whether trustee exemption clauses should be subject to some regulation. We conclude that there is a problem that needs to be addressed and that we are particularly concerned by the incidence of trustee exemption provisions where the settlor does not fully understand their meaning and effect. However, we warn that any reform must take account of the desirability of retaining settler autonomy and have regard to its impact on beneficiaries and the wider consequences of regulation. In Part 4, we consider whether any regulation should make a distinction between "professional" and "lay" trustees. We conclude that a better approach is to make a distinction on the basis of receipt of remuneration (that is, whether the trustee is paid or unpaid). In Part 5, we review the CP's provisional proposals in light of the responses received during the consultation process, and we explain our reasons for rejecting legislative reform of the sort favoured in the CP. In Part 6, we consider the case for alternative forms of regulation, dealing specifically with the problem of settlor awareness. We explain the practice-based approach we now recommend, and set out a statement of a rule of practice which we commend to regulatory and professional bodies whose members act as trustees or draft trust instruments.

1.30 In Appendix A, we review a number of options for reform discussed but provisionally rejected in the CP. In Appendix B, we consider the relationship

---

[17] STEP's rule is reproduced in Appendix G.

between trustee indemnity insurance and trustee exemption clauses. In Appendix C, we outline the arguments made in the course of consultation for the different treatment of three specific types of trust: charitable trusts, pension trusts and commercial trusts. In Appendix D, we give further consideration to the difficulties surrounding so-called duty modification clauses. In Appendix E, we set out certain statistics about trusts.

1.31   We are very grateful to all who responded to the CP whose names are listed in Appendix H. As explained in a press release dated 14 December 2005, we have, since the consultation period ended, engaged in further, extremely helpful, discussions about a non-statutory approach to regulation with a number of bodies capable of influencing practice within this area. The organisations with whom we have met are listed in Appendix F. At the time of publication of this Report, the England and Wales region of STEP has already approved a rule of practice of its own which will apply to its membership. This rule is set out in Appendix G.

1.32   We wish to record the considerable support given to the Law Commission by STEP, both its assistance with the organisation of conferences and seminars, and in discussions concerning the non-statutory approach that we are now recommending. In particular, we thank Charles Gothard, Geoffrey Shindler and Simon Jennings. We are also grateful to the Wills and Equity Committee of the Law Society and to the Institute of Chartered Accountants in England and Wales for their efforts.

1.33   Finally, we wish to record our continued gratitude to the Trust Law Committee. The TLC was instrumental in raising the issue of regulation of trustee exemption clauses following the decision in *Armitage v Nurse*,[18] and its members have given freely of their time throughout this project. We are particularly indebted to its Chairman, Sir Peter Gibson, the Honourable Mr Justice David Hayton (of the Caribbean Court of Justice), John Dilger, Professor Paul Matthews and its former Chairman, the late Sir John Vinelott.

---

[18]   [1998] Ch 241.

PART 2
THE CURRENT LAW[1]

WHAT ARE TRUSTEE EXEMPTION CLAUSES?

2.1 A trustee exemption clause[2] is a clause in a trust instrument which purports to exclude or restrict the trustee's liability for failure to carry out properly the duties imposed upon it by the trust instrument or by law.

2.2 In addition to clauses that seek simply to exclude or restrict liability for breach of trust, there are various other types of clause which purport to secure exemption from liability. These consist of clauses which limit the scope of the trustees' duties ("duty modification clauses"), clauses which extend the trustee's powers ("extended powers clauses") and clauses which entitle the trustee to indemnity from the trust fund ("indemnity clauses").

BREACH OF TRUST

2.3 A breach of trust is a breach of any obligation owed by the trustee. Such obligations may be imposed expressly by the trust instrument or impliedly by law. As Millett LJ explained in *Armitage v Nurse*:

> Breaches of trust are of many different kinds. A breach of trust may be deliberate or inadvertent; it may consist of an actual misappropriation or misapplication of the trust property or merely of an investment or other dealing which is outside the trustees' powers; it may consist of a failure to carry out a positive obligation of the trustees or merely of a want of skill and care on their part in the management of the trust property; it may be injurious to the interests of the beneficiaries or be actually to their benefit.[3]

Breach of fiduciary duty

2.4 Trustees stand in a fiduciary relationship with their beneficiaries and as such are subject to the fiduciary obligation of loyalty. From the fundamental obligation of loyalty there have evolved specific duties which trustees must observe. These duties are that trustees:

(1) must act in good faith;[4]

(2) must not make an unauthorised profit from their trust;[5]

(3) must not place themselves in a position where their duty and interest conflict;[6] and

---

[1] For a fuller exposition of the current law, see Part II of the CP.

[2] The term is used interchangeably with "trustee exoneration clause" and "trustee exculpation clause".

[3] *Armitage v Nurse* [1998] Ch 241, 251.

[4] *Re Second East Dulwich* (1899) 68 LJ Ch 196.

[5] *Bray v Ford* [1896] AC 44.

(4)   must not act for their own benefit or for the benefit of a third party, without the informed consent of the beneficiaries of the trust.[7]

Breach of duty of care

2.5   The most common breach of duty occurs where a trustee breaches its duty to act with care and skill in the administration of the trust, thereby causing loss to the trust fund. This duty of care may be imposed by statute or by common law.[8] The duty of care is not a fiduciary duty as such and should therefore be distinguished from those duties, peculiar to fiduciaries, which are mentioned above.[9]

2.6   The statutory duty of care introduced by the Trustee Act 2000 applies to the exercise of powers and the performance of duties conferred or imposed by that Act, as well as to certain powers conferred by other statutes and powers conferred by the terms of the trust.[10] It is not, however, of general application. The duty of care "under the general law" applies therefore to those powers and duties that are not expressly covered by the Trustee Act 2000.

Negligence not necessary

2.7   It is important to emphasise that liability for breach of trust is not restricted to acts or omissions which can be characterised as negligent. Where trustees act outside the powers conferred upon them (*ultra vires*), it is not necessary for a claimant beneficiary to prove negligence. As has been stated by one commentator, there is as a result in the law of trusts:

> ... a strong element of strict liability in the sense of liability which is not dependent on showing negligence or unreasonableness on the part of the trustee.[11]

THE LEADING CASE

2.8   The Court of Appeal in *Armitage v Nurse*[12] held that in English law trustee exemption clauses can validly exempt trustees from liability for all breaches of trust except fraud.

2.9   In *Armitage v Nurse*, the settled property consisted largely of land farmed by a company, the directors of which were the mother and grandmother of the claimant beneficiary ("B"). Under the settlement, B was contingently entitled to her share of the fund at the age of 40. Following a substantial fall in the value of the land, B claimed that the trustees were in breach of trust as regards the

---

[6]   *Keech v Sandford* (1726) 2 Eq Cas Abr 741.

[7]   *Boardman v Phipps* [1967] 2 AC 46.

[8]   *Bartlett v Barclays Bank Trust Co Ltd (Nos 1 & 2)* [1980] Ch 515. For the statutory duty of care, see Trustee Act 2000, s 1.

[9]   *Lewin on Trusts* (17th ed 2000) para 34-01.

[10]   For the cases where the statutory duty applies, see Trustee Act 2000, s 2 and sch 1.

[11]   R Ham QC, "Trustees' Liability" (1995) 9 *Trust Law International* 21, at 21.

[12]   [1998] Ch 241.

management and investment of the fund, as a result of which substantial loss had been caused.

2.10   Clause 15 of the settlement in *Armitage v Nurse* provided that:

> No trustee shall be liable for any loss or damage which may happen to [B]'s fund or any part thereof or the income thereof at any time or from any cause whatsoever unless such loss or damage shall be caused by his own actual fraud... .

2.11   The Court held that clause 15 was effective to exempt a trustee from liability for loss or damage to the trust property "no matter how indolent, imprudent, lacking in diligence, negligent or wilful he may have been, so long as he has not acted dishonestly".[13] It was contended by B that the word "fraud" in clause 15 included equitable fraud,[14] but this contention was rejected by the Court. Construing clause 15, Millett LJ considered that the word "actual" had been deliberately used to exclude equitable fraud.[15] He held that "actual fraud" required proof of dishonesty, and he accepted a formulation put forward by counsel for the trustees to the effect that fraud in this context:

> ... connotes at the minimum an intention on the part of the trustee to pursue a particular course of action, either knowing that it is contrary to the interests of the beneficiaries or being recklessly indifferent whether it is contrary to their interests or not.[16]

2.12   Claims by B that the clause was void for repugnancy or contrary to public policy were rejected. Reviewing the nineteenth century authorities which, it was contended, underpinned B's argument, Millett LJ held that *Wilkins v Hogg*[17] had decided that an appropriately worded clause could limit the scope of the trustee liability in any way the settlor chose. He also held that the statement of Bacon VC in *Pass v Dundas*[18] that an exemption clause only protected trustees from liability in the absence of proof of gross negligence was not necessary for the decision in that case (*obiter*). Of the Scottish authorities he concluded that:

> ... none of them are authority for the proposition that it is contrary to public policy to exclude liability for gross negligence by an appropriate clause clearly worded to have that effect.[19]

---

[13]   [1998] Ch 241, 251.

[14]   "Equitable fraud...covers breach of fiduciary duty, undue influence, abuse of confidence, unconscionable bargains and frauds on powers. With the sole exception of the last, which is a technical doctrine in which the word 'fraud' merely connotes excess of vires, it involves some dealing by the fiduciary with his principal and the risk that the fiduciary may have exploited his position to his own advantage." [1998] Ch 241, 252-253, per Millett LJ.

[15]   [1998] Ch 241, 250.

[16]   [1998] Ch 241, 251.

[17]   (1861) 31 LJ Ch 41. See CP, para 2.27.

[18]   (1880) 43 LT 665. See CP, para 2.29.

[19]   [1998] Ch 241, 256.

2.13   The approach advocated by Millett LJ requires the court to construe the words of the exemption clause in the light of the conduct complained of and to decide whether any potential liability has been effectively excluded by the terms of the trust. In carrying out this exercise, while the court should construe the clause restrictively, it must do so fairly, according to the natural meaning of the words used.[20] Liability can therefore be excluded only by clear, unequivocal and unambiguous terms.[21] However, it should be borne in mind that the trust instrument has been created by the settlor, not by the trustees acting as such. Accordingly, a strict *contra proferentem* approach is not justified.[22]

2.14   Although *Armitage v Nurse* gives considerable latitude to the use of trustee exemption clauses, the line is drawn at actual fraud, on the basis that to permit a trustee to act dishonestly would be to derogate from the "irreducible core of obligations"[23] of honesty and good faith. A trust instrument which allowed the trustee to act fraudulently without giving the beneficiaries any recourse would fail as a trust. Millett LJ rejected the contention that the trustee's duty of skill, care, prudence and diligence was one of the irreducible core obligations of the trust.

2.15   It must be admitted that the authority of *Armitage v Nurse* (as a decision of the Court of Appeal not the House of Lords) is not entirely free from doubt. The view taken by Millett LJ of the nineteenth century Scottish cases does not accord with the understanding of these decisions north of the border, where it is generally believed that trustees cannot invoke an exemption clause to escape liability for gross negligence, or, as it is there termed, *culpa lata*.[24] While there is no reason why the English and Scottish law should be identical in this respect, the reliance placed by Millett LJ on the Scottish cases was clearly an important part of his reasoning, and should that reliance be shown to have been misplaced, the authority of the decision may be called into question.

2.16   However, as a result of the decision in *Armitage v Nurse* it appears now to be the settled law in England and Wales that trustee exemption clauses can validly exempt trustees from all breaches of trust except where such breaches were fraudulent or dishonest.

OTHER LITIGATION

2.17   The Court of Appeal has been asked to consider issues relating to exemption clauses in trust instruments on a number of occasions since its decision in *Armitage v Nurse*.

---

[20]   *Bogg v Raper* (1998/99) 1 ITELR 267, 281.

[21]   *Midland Bank Trustee (Jersey) Ltd v Federated Pension Services Ltd* [1996] PLR 179, 192; *Armitage v Nurse* [1998] Ch 241, 255; *Bogg v Raper* (1998/99) 1 ITELR 267, 280; and *Wight v Olswang (No 2)* (1999/2000) 2 ITELR 689.

[22]   *Bogg v Raper* (1998/99) 1 ITELR 267, 281. See also the discussion of this issue by the Jersey Court of Appeal in *Midland Bank Trustee (Jersey) Ltd v Federated Pension Services Ltd* [1996] PLR 179, 192.

[23]   *Armitage v Nurse* [1998] Ch 241, 253.

[24]   *Lutea Trustees Ltd v Orbis Trustees Guernsey Ltd* 1998 SLT 471.

Bogg v Raper

2.18　In *Bogg v Raper*,[25] the Court of Appeal considered whether these principles of construction were applicable where the trustees seeking exemption from liability had been involved in the creation of the settlement containing the trustee exemption clause. A will trust comprised shares which represented a controlling interest in a private limited company. Beneficiaries claimed that the trustees failed to exercise proper control over the business and the activities of the company, thereby causing loss to the trust. However, the trustees successfully argued that they were protected by the exemption in clause 12 of the will, which provided:

> In the professed execution of the trusts and powers hereof, no trustees (other than a trust corporation) shall be liable for any loss to the trust premises arising by reason of any improper investment made in good faith...or by reason of any mistake or omission made in good faith...by any trustee hereof or by reason of any other matter or thing except wilful or individual fraud or wrongdoing on the part of the trustee who is sought to be made liable.

2.19　The trustees, being the testator's solicitor and accountant, were responsible for the inclusion of the exemption clause in the will. The Court rejected the argument that this should prevent them from relying on the clause on the basis that they would be deriving a benefit from a breach of their fiduciary duty to the testator (not to put themselves in a position of conflict of interest and duty). Millett LJ held that an exemption clause of the sort contained in clause 12 of the will did not confer a benefit on the trustees, but simply defined the extent of their liability. In so far as a benefit was conferred, it was a benefit which could be enjoyed by any person assuming the role of trustee in relation to the trust and was not exclusive to those who had participated in the preparation of the testator's will.

2.20　This aspect of *Bogg v Raper* has been criticised on the ground that the solicitor did obtain a benefit in saving the expense of insurance premiums which would otherwise have been payable to protect him from liability.[26]

Wight v Olswang (No 2)

2.21　The trust instrument in *Wight v Olswang (No 2)*[27] contained two inconsistent exemption clauses. One was limited in its application to trustees not charging remuneration for acting; the other was not. The Court held that this disparity created an ambiguity and the trustees were not protected from liability by either clause.

Walker v Stones

2.22　The Court of Appeal was asked to consider the meaning of "fraud" in *Walker v Stones*.[28] The Court held that where a solicitor-trustee honestly believed that he

---

[25]　(1998/99) 1 ITELR 267.

[26]　Hayton & Marshall, *The Law of Trusts and Equitable Remedies* (11th ed 2001) para 9-311. See also cases cited at para 9-310: *Baskerville v Thurgood* (1992) 100 Sask LR 214 and *Rutanen v Ballard* (1997) 424 Mass 723, 733.

[27]　(1999/2000) 2 ITELR 689.

[28]　[2001] QB 902.

was acting in the best interests of the trust, his actions could nevertheless be held to be fraudulent if no reasonable solicitor-trustee would have thought that what was done was for the benefit of the beneficiaries.[29]

2.23 In *Armitage v Nurse*,[30] Millett LJ explained that "actual fraud", in the context of the exemption clause in that case, "simply means dishonesty".[31] The approach to the question of dishonesty in *Walker v Stones*[32] (an objective examination of the defendant's conduct in the light of his subjective knowledge at the time) appears to follow that of the Privy Council in *Royal Brunei Airlines Sdn Bhd v Tan*.[33] That *Royal Brunei Airlines*[34] takes the correct approach to dishonesty has recently been confirmed, in the context of dishonest assistance in breach of trust, in *Barlow Clowes International Ltd (In Liquidation) v Eurotrust International Ltd*.[35]

2.24 How the courts will reconcile the fragmented interpretations of what "dishonesty" requires in the various trust law contexts remains to be seen.[36]

Further developments

2.25 Since the publication of the CP in January 2003, there have been no substantive developments relating to the permissible content of trustee exemption clauses. The scope of exemption clauses has been considered in a number of pensions cases, but these have concerned questions of construction rather than of the underlying trust law.[37]

2.26 Two recent cases have considered trustee exemption clauses:

(1) In *Barraclough v Mell*,[38] Judge Behrens accepted and applied[39] the current law as described in the CP.[40]

(2) In *Baker v JE Clark & Co (Transport) UK Ltd*,[41] the Court of Appeal upheld a trustee exemption clause[42] and emphasised the unilateral

---

[29] *Walker v Stones* [2001] QB 902, 941.

[30] [1998] Ch 241.

[31] *Armitage v Nurse* [1998] 2 Ch 241, 251.

[32] [2001] QB 902.

[33] [1995] 2 AC 378.

[34] *Royal Brunei Airlines Sdn Bhd v Tan* [1995] 2 AC 378.

[35] [2005] UKPC 37, [2006] 1 All ER 333.

[36] The precise meaning of "dishonesty" for trust law purposes lies outside the scope of the current project.

[37] See *Elliott v Pensions Ombudsman* [1998] OPLR 21; *Woodland-Ferrari v UCL Group Retirement Benefits Scheme* [2002] EWHC 1354 (Ch), [2003] Ch 115; *Seifert v Pensions Ombudsman* [1997] 4 All ER 947; *Duckitt v Pensions Ombudsman* [2000] OPLR 167 and *Alexander Forbes Trustee Services Ltd v Halliwell* [2003] EWHC 1685 (Ch), [2003] Pens LR 269.

[38] [2005] EWHC 3387 (Ch), [2006] WTLR 203.

[39] [2005] EWHC 3387 (Ch), [2006] WTLR 203, at [90] and following.

[40] CP, p vii.

[41] *Baker v JE Clark & Co (Transport) UK Ltd* [2006] EWCA Civ 464, judgment of 22 March 2006, Court of Appeal (unreported).

nature of the obligations arising from the trust relationship.[43] The appellant's attempt to circumvent the exemption clause by claiming that the trustee owed a common law duty of care to the beneficiaries which was outside of the trust itself and therefore not affected by the clause was rejected.[44] Furthermore, the Court rejected the appellant's claim that a trustee exemption clause could be subjected to the reasonableness test in the Unfair Contract Terms Act 1977.[45]

STATUTORY CONTROLS

2.27 There are three sets of statutory provisions which may impact on trustee exemption clauses in the contexts of financial services, companies and pensions.

Financial Services and Markets Act 2000

2.28 Section 253 of the Financial Services and Markets Act 2000 provides that:

> Any provision of the trust deed of an authorised unit trust scheme is void in so far as it would have the effect of exempting the manager or trustee from liability for any failure to exercise due care and diligence in the discharge of his functions in respect of the scheme.

2.29 Consequently, trustees of a unit trust scheme which is authorised by the Financial Services Authority cannot rely on any clause contained in the scheme's trust deed which has the effect of exempting them from liability for negligence.

Companies Act 1985

2.30 Section 192(1) of the Companies Act 1985 provides that:

> Subject to this section, any provision contained –
>
> (a) in a trust deed for the issue of debentures, or

---

[42] The clause excluded liability for mistakes made by the trustees, except where they had acted in bad faith.

[43] The Court expressly rejected the appellant's suggestion that the exemption clause could only be relied upon if it had been "incorporated" into the relationship between trustee and beneficiary by the beneficiary being made aware of it, and stressed that "trustees undertake unilateral obligations and are entitled to limit the extent of the duties they assume": *Baker v JE Clark & Co (Transport) UK Ltd* [2006] EWCA Civ 464, judgment of 22 March 2006, Court of Appeal (unreported) at [17], per Tuckey LJ.

[44] Tuckey LJ appeared to rule out the possibility of ever finding that a trustee owed a common law duty outside of the trust (and therefore not susceptible to a trustee exemption clause): "There is therefore no basis for saying that [the trustee] assumed some super-added common law or equitable duty of care, even if in such circumstances on other facts it was possible to spell out such a duty, which I doubt." *Baker v JE Clark & Co (Transport) UK Ltd* [2006] EWCA Civ 464, judgment of 22 March 2006, Court of Appeal (unreported) at [16].

[45] Tuckey LJ accepted that the appellant was right to concede that a trust is not a "contract" for the purpose of the Unfair Contract Terms Act, ss 1-2, and held, referring to paragraphs 2.62 and 4.45 of the CP, that a trust is also not a "notice" for this purpose.

(b) in any contract with the holders of debentures secured by a trust deed,

is void in so far as it would have the effect of exempting a trustee of the deed from, or indemnifying him against, liability for breach of trust where he fails to show the degree of care and diligence required of him as trustee, having regard to the provisions of the trust deed conferring on him any powers, authorities or discretions.[46]

2.31　Section 310 of the Companies Act 1985 renders void:

… any provision, whether contained in a company's articles or in any contract with the company or otherwise, for exempting…any person (whether an officer or not) employed by the company as auditor from, or indemnifying him against, any liability…in respect of…breach of trust…in relation to the company.[47]

Pensions Act 1995

2.32　The duties of pension trustees are already supplemented by obligations and requirements imposed by the Pensions Act 1995. Section 33(1) provides that:

Liability for breach of an obligation under any rule of law to take care or exercise skill in the performance of any investment functions, where the function is exercisable –

(a) by a trustee of a trust scheme, or

(b) by a person to whom the function has been delegated under section 34,

cannot be excluded or restricted by any instrument or agreement.

CHARITABLE TRUSTS

2.33　The general law relating to the scope and validity of exemption clauses applies equally to charitable trusts, and therefore an exemption clause similar to that upheld in *Armitage v Nurse* could in principle be included in the governing instrument of a charity.[48]

---

[46]　See Financial Markets Law Committee, *Trustee Exemption Clauses Report – Issue 62* (May 2004) p 3 for discussion of the meaning of this provision.

[47]　For exceptions, see Companies Act 1985, s 310(3).

[48]　An example of the type of exclusion clause used in charitable trust deeds can be found in *Butterworth's Encyclopaedia of Forms and Precedents* (5th ed 2001 Reissue) vol 6(2), p 115:

In the execution of the trusts and powers of this Deed no Trustee shall be liable for any loss to the Charity arising by reason of any improper investment made in good faith (so long as he shall have sought professional advice before making such investment) or any mistake or omission made in good faith by him or any other Trustee or any other matter other than wilful and individual fraud wrongdoing or wrongful omission on the part of the Trustee who is sought to be made liable.

2.34 The powers of charity trustees are found in their trust instrument, the general trust law and statutes, notably the Trustee Acts of 1925 and 2000. The duties of charity trustees are more or less the same as trustees of private non-charitable funds.[49] However, trustees of charitable funds have additional duties and administrative controls imposed by the Charities Acts of 1992 and 1993.[50] Clause 39 of the Charities Bill will give charitable trustees a default power to purchase indemnity insurance.[51]

Incorporated charities

2.35 Many charities are established as limited companies. Nonetheless, the duties which are imposed on such persons as trustees by the general law and by the Charities Acts are fully binding and unaffected by any limited liability which that incorporation may otherwise incur.[52]

2.36 Section 310 of the Companies Act 1985 has particular significance in relation to trustees of an incorporated charity.[53] One effect of this provision is to create an inequality between those charities which are incorporated and those which are not. In the latter case, trustee exemption clauses are only constrained by the requirements of good faith and honesty expounded by Millett LJ in *Armitage v Nurse*.[54]

Exemption clauses and exclusively charitable purposes

2.37 It is open to argument that an exemption clause in a charitable trust which does not fall foul of the general *Armitage v Nurse* criteria might nevertheless be invalid as being incompatible with the requirement of exclusively charitable purposes because it confers a private benefit on trustees. However, such argument may fail if the court were to adopt the approach of Millett LJ in *Bogg v Raper*,[55] that they are to be considered not as conferring a benefit on the trustees, but merely as laying down the extent of their potential liability.

2.38 It is understood from the Charity Commission that wide "duty exclusion" clauses are rarely encountered. More common are clauses which prescribe a lower standard of care for charity trustees than that which would otherwise be applied by the general law. There is no decided case which considers the compatibility of such clauses with the principle that a charity has to be established for exclusively

---

[49] See *Tudor on Charities* (8th ed 1995) p 244.

[50] Such as the duty to apply for registration as a charity, to prepare and submit annual returns to the Charity Commission, to retain accounting records for at least six years and generally to comply with the rules for the preparation of annual accounts and their submission to the Charity Commission.

[51] See further Appendix B, paras B.39 and following.

[52] In *Re French Protestant Hospital* [1951] Ch 567, 571, Danckwerts J said:

> ... [directors] who are already in the same position of trustees, and therefore, so far as they exercise their powers at all, bound to exercise them in a fiduciary manner on behalf of the charitable trusts for which they act... .

[53] See para 2.31.

[54] Leaving aside the "exclusively charitable" considerations, on which see paras 2.37 to 2.38.

[55] (1998/99) 1 ITELR 267.

charitable purposes, nor have the Charity Commissioners explicitly considered the point.

SUMMARY

2.39   Unless or until the efficacy of trustee exemption clauses is argued before the House of Lords, the current English law is to be found in the judgment of Millett LJ in *Armitage v Nurse*. A trustee exemption clause may exempt a trustee from liability for all acts, omissions or breaches of trust save where the trustee has committed actual fraud. It is therefore possible for a settlor to create an effective trust which does not impose on the trustee a duty to take reasonable care. Even gross negligence on the part of the trustee may not result in legal liability in the event of a widely drawn exemption clause. Only if the instrument seeks to free the trustees from the core obligations of honesty and good faith will it fail as a trust.

PART 3
THE CASE FOR REFORM

SHOULD TRUSTEE EXEMPTION CLAUSES BE REGULATED?

3.1 In this Part we re-examine whether it is necessary to introduce some regulation of trustee exemption clauses. This is the principal question faced in this project. There is, however, an important subsidiary question. If it is considered that regulation of trustee exemption clauses is necessary, should that regulation be effected by legislation or by some other means?

3.2 During consultation, we sought the views of consultees on the desirability of legislative regulation. In the CP, having rejected an outright prohibition of trustee exemption clauses, we considered "… that some legislative regulation of trustee exemption clauses is justified and necessary".[1] We asked consultees whether they agreed with this proposition. Nearly three quarters of consultees did so.

3.3 This headline figure should not, however, be allowed to disguise the extent of opposition to legislative regulation and the serious concerns that were expressed to us about reform of this sort. There was particular unease about the potential for legislative regulation to give rise to adverse consequences. While some consultees considered that risk to be manageable (and so supported legislative intervention), others believed these problems to be inescapable (and so opposed reform).

3.4 As this Report makes clear, the impact of reform depends very much on the model of regulation proposed. We therefore do not discuss the potential for adverse consequences any further at this stage. We shall return to the issue when discussing particular models of regulation.[2] This Part will only consider the *prima facie* case for reform.

3.5 Consultees' detailed responses about the necessity for legislative intervention addressed two distinct issues. First, they considered the principled arguments about the propriety of trustee exemption clauses. Secondly, they commented on whether the extent of reliance on trustee exemption clauses was sufficient to require reform.

IS THERE A PROBLEM?

3.6 The "problem" posed by trustee exemption clauses is not one of legal uncertainty. The decision of the Court of Appeal in *Armitage v Nurse*[3] put the question of how far trustees are currently able to rely on exemption clauses largely beyond doubt. The simple issue is whether or not the current law is fair. Does the freedom of the trustee to rely upon trustee exemption clauses accord insufficient protection to the interests of those for whose benefit the trust relationship exists? Or does it

---

[1]   CP, para 4.20.

[2]   See paras 5.12 to 5.37, and paras 6.11 to 6.40.

[3]   [1998] Ch 241.

represent an acceptable balance between the interests of settlor, beneficiary and trustee?

3.7 The CP concluded that "the current law is too deferential to trustees".[4] This position echoes the "widely held" view reported by Millett LJ in *Armitage v Nurse* that "these clauses have gone too far".[5] It reflects the conclusions of the Trust Law Committee's consultation paper[6] on trustee exemption clauses that the current law is in need of reform.

Support for reform

3.8 In the course of consultation, there was widespread agreement that the use of trustee exemption clauses has reduced the protection afforded to beneficiaries in the event of breach of trust to an unacceptably low level. Consultees generally supported the CP's suggestion that the law is consequently too deferential to trustees (in particular, professional trustees) and that reform is necessary in order to rectify the imbalance. Some consultees expressed particular distaste for the tendency of some trustees to insist on wide trustee exemption clauses automatically without any regard to the circumstances of the particular trust. Many considered the problem especially acute where the settlor is unaware of the existence, meaning or effect of the relevant clause at the time of execution of the trust instrument.

3.9 A number of consultees contrasted the extent to which trustees are currently permitted to rely on exemption clauses with other areas of private law. In particular, comparisons were drawn with the operation of the Unfair Contract Terms Act 1977 which permits the exclusion of liability for negligence by a contractual term only in so far as the term satisfies the requirement of reasonableness.[7]

3.10 However, disparity with other areas of the law did not appear to be the prime concern. Most of the consultees who contended that legislative regulation was necessary appeared to disapprove instinctively of trustee exemption clauses, considering them inherently objectionable.

Objections to reform

3.11 Despite the apparently strong overall support for reform, consultees[8] raised a number of concerns. Many of the arguments against reform criticised the view that the current law unduly favours trustees over beneficiaries, on the basis that it fails to recognise the true nature of a trust as a tripartite relationship between settlors, trustees and beneficiaries.

---

[4] CP, para 4.20.

[5] *Armitage v Nurse* [1998] Ch 241, 256.

[6] Trust Law Committee, *Consultation Paper: Trustee Exemption Clauses* (June 1999).

[7] Unfair Contract Terms Act 1977, s 2.

[8] Including consultees who agreed with the provisional proposal that there should be reform.

Proper protection of trustees

3.12 Consultees contended that there are circumstances in which it may be perfectly reasonable for trustees to expect greater protection.

3.13 This may be the case because of the circumstances of the trusteeship or because of the nature of the trust assets. The Chancery Bar Association labelled these as "warring factions" and "difficult assets" cases, and put forward the following examples:

(1) A testator's will grants his widow a life interest in the estate with remainder to his children by a previous marriage. If there is hostility between the children and the step-mother, the trustee may be in a difficult and potentially risky position. It may be legitimate for that trustee to shield itself from the "warring factions" by invocation of a trustee exemption clause. Although a court may be slow to find negligence in such a case, the trustee still needs the comfort of a trustee exemption clause to be able to act decisively, and may be reluctant to take on the trusteeship without one.

(2) Shares in a private company have been settled on trust with the intention that they should be retained as the principal trust asset. An exemption clause[9] would protect the trustees against accusations that they failed to sell the shares and diversify the investments of the trust fund.[10]

3.14 Attention was also drawn to the standard use of exemption provisions in many commercial trusts. Consultees explained that the extent of risk, the involvement of other parties and the passive functions of the trustee made exemption provisions a prerequisite for the use of trusts in such structures.[11]

3.15 If it is accepted that trustee exemption provisions play an important and legitimate role in specific circumstances it would be unfair to deny trustees the protection afforded by them in such cases.

Infringement of settlor's autonomy

3.16 It is indisputable that any regulation of exemption clauses would limit the rights of the settlor as well as those of the trustee. The terms of a trust are determined by the settlor disposing of his or her assets. It is therefore the settlor who is responsible for the inclusion of exemption provisions for the protection of the trustee.

3.17 A number of consultees argued that any legislative restriction of reliance on trustee exemption clauses would constitute an unjustified infringement of the freedom of settlors to dispose of their property on whatever terms they thought fit. For example, one consultee asked "if the settlor has chosen to give his trustee the benefit of an exemption clause, after being fully informed of the issues

---

[9] Or a duty modification clause having the effect of excluding liability for negligence. See further para 5.46 and following, and Appendix D.

[10] Other examples of "difficult assets" given by consultees included trusts to hold paintings, agricultural land and family heirlooms.

[11] See further Appendix C, para C.33 and following.

involved and thereafter giving his informed consent, why should Parliament intervene?"[12] Another argued that "a trust is created by persons who are, by definition, adults who are *compos mentis* and acting voluntarily. The law should stand back a long way before imposing any restrictions on their freedom of action."[13]

3.18 To some extent, the vindication of exemption clauses in *Armitage v Nurse* can be presented as a triumph of the autonomy of the settlor above the expectations of beneficiaries. Regulation that restricted trustees' ability to rely on such clauses would, it may be argued, promote the interests of beneficiaries above those of settlors. In the majority of cases, where benefits are granted gratuitously, the effect would be to favour the recipients of bounty above its source.

3.19 Consultees pointed out that many settlors are content and even eager to grant their trustees exemption. This may be for personal reasons; for example, to protect a family member or friend who is the intended trustee from potential personal loss. Alternatively, settlors may agree to a request for an exemption clause where this ensures a reduction in the annual fee that would otherwise apply or where necessary to obtain the services of a preferred trustee.

3.20 The settlor autonomy argument was not, however, without its critics. A number of consultees pointed out that trustee exemption clauses are commonly included in trust instruments as a matter of routine. In some cases, the clauses form part of a "take-it-or-leave-it" package put forward by trustees. If it is true that the modern settlor who wants to use a professional trustee is forced to agree to an exemption clause, it is more difficult to characterise its consequent inclusion in the trust instrument as an autonomous exercise. The same applies if the clause is hidden away in "boilerplate" administrative provisions which the settlor is unlikely to read, let alone comprehend.

3.21 Other consultees suggested that certain fetters on autonomy should be accepted in the same way as freedom to contract is limited by consumer-protection legislation. It was pointed out that there is a stronger argument for limiting the autonomy of a settlor than a contracting party, because a trust gives rise to fiduciary duties and it is to non-contracting parties (the beneficiaries) that those duties are owed. It should also be borne in mind that, as *Armitage v Nurse* confirmed, there are already some restrictions on settlors' ability to exempt trustees from liability, so the question is one of extent.[14]

Impact on beneficiaries

3.22 A number of consultees suggested that it is simplistic to view the interests of the trustee and the beneficiary as being wholly opposed. Many argued that it was often in the wider interests of beneficiaries for trusts to include an exemption

---

[12] Geoffrey Shindler, Lane-Smith and Shindler LLP, Vice-president of the Society of Trust and Estate Practitioners.

[13] M Jacobs, "Trustee Exemption Clauses: Another view" (June 2003) *Trusts and Estates Law Journal* 8

[14] Aside from the "core obligations" identified in *Armitage v Nurse*, certain categories of property are made inalienable by statute or by reason of public policy and a trust created for a purpose illegal under English law will be void.

clause. Many of the potential adverse consequences of regulation discussed in Part 5[15] would impact on the size of the trust fund or the efficient administration of the trust. These outcomes would not necessarily favour beneficiaries at the expense of trustees.

3.23 Of course, this argument only goes so far. However great the indirect advantages exemption clauses may offer beneficiaries as a class, there is clearly a net loss to individual beneficiaries where all or part of a particular trust fund is irrecoverably lost through trustee negligence. As soon as a breach of trust arises, the interests of the beneficiaries and the trustee are in direct conflict. If the trustee is then able to escape liability at the expense of the beneficiaries, the trustee's interests will have prevailed.

Specific trust markets

3.24 A number of consultees were of the view that there is no need for trustee exemption clause reform in relation to certain types of trust.

3.25 For example, several argued that the beneficiaries under commercial trusts do not require the same protection as the beneficiaries of family trusts, as the former are almost always the market equals of their trustees. As many of consultees' concerns about the effect of regulation on commercial trusts were targeted at the specific scheme provisionally proposed in the CP, we do not reproduce them here. However, a fuller discussion of the appropriateness of regulation in the commercial trust sphere is set out in Appendix C.

3.26 Consultees also presented a range of arguments about the need for regulation of trustee exemption clauses in pension trusts and charitable trusts. These are also described at Appendix C.

Summary

3.27 We acknowledge that there are a number of grounds for opposing the wide regulation of reliance on trustee exemption clauses. The answer to the question of whether the current law is unjust is not, however, as clear-cut as many would suggest. On balance, we remain of the view that the current law governing trustee exemption clauses is capable of causing unfairness and should be addressed. However, the arguments against reform clearly need to be borne in mind when considering the appropriate means of regulation.

EXTENT OF THE PROBLEM

3.28 Even if it is accepted that there is a problem, it is necessary to assess its extent before settling on an appropriate solution. It must be shown that the creation of and reliance on trustee exemption clauses is sufficiently widespread to warrant intervention.

3.29 The nature of trusts makes any assessment of such matters far from straightforward. The CP noted several obstacles facing those attempting to obtain

---

[15] For example, a rise in trustee fees or insurance premiums taken directly from the trust, an increase in operational costs, delays in decision making and a reluctance to exercise discretions without prior legal advice (see para 5.12 and following).

information about trustee exemption clauses in particular and trusts in general. Trusts are an institution of private law and, in most cases, form a private arrangement between a settlor and one or more trustees. Trusts are not publicly recorded and there is no general requirement to register them. We have attempted to gather statistics about trusts from the Inland Revenue, the Charity Commission and the Probate Registry.[16] However, none of these organisations is able to provide comprehensive figures.

3.30   This is only the first level of difficulty. Even if authoritative figures for the number of trusts in England and Wales did exist, such figures would not indicate the frequency of exemption clauses within those trusts, still less the content of those clauses.

3.31   This lack of publicly available data prompted the Commission, before publishing the CP, to instruct Dr Alison Dunn's socio-economic research on the use of trustee exemption clauses. The methodology and findings of the research are set out in Part III of the CP.

3.32   Dr Dunn's study included a consideration of the prevalence of trustee exemption clauses in practice. As the CP reported, respondents to questionnaires and interviewees thought that trustee exemption clauses were very frequently included in trust instruments. Although trustee respondents indicated that fewer than half of their trusts contained an exemption clause, clauses were much more commonly experienced by trust professionals. Legal adviser respondents considered exemption clauses very common, a substantial majority believing that most trusts contained one.

3.33   It was suggested during consultation that little weight should be attached to the research findings, as the low response rates to the survey invalidated any conclusions that could be drawn from it.[17] The CP had acknowledged that the levels of response meant that "the results of the questionnaires cannot be regarded as representative of the group taken as a whole and therefore must be treated with some caution".[18] In particular, there is the danger that those who were willing to participate "self-selected" themselves on account of strongly-held views. That said, the research was helpful in indicating trends within current trust practice, and the interviews that took place were useful in providing an account of the experience of those operating in the field.

3.34   Another possible indicator of the prevalence of trustee exemption clauses is their use in trust precedents. Trustee exemption clauses do feature in many precedents published for the assistance of those drafting trust instruments.[19] However, that is not to say that all precedents advocate the use of such provisions. For example, Kessler's *Drafting Trusts and Will Trusts* suggests that

---

[16]   The results are set out in Appendix E.

[17]   The study's quantitative research (carried out through questionnaires) achieved only a 13% response rate among trustees and a 17% rate among legal advisers. See CP, paras 3.10 and 3.15.

[18]   CP, para 3.15.

[19]   See CP, para 3.19.

"the most respected textbooks"[20] support the view that "the blanket exemption clause has no place in a standard [trust]".[21] Reference is made to the guidance of, amongst others, Prideaux (who provides a draft clause but advises that it should only be used in special circumstances[22]) and the authors of the *Encyclopaedia of Forms and Precedents* (who note, in the 2001 edition, that the clause should not be used by professional trustees and that "it is essential that the settlor is made fully aware of how the clause operates and agrees to its inclusion"[23]). Kessler nevertheless acknowledges that "some firms are unwilling to listen to that note of caution, and insert the widest possible trustee exemption clauses for the benefit of themselves as professional trustees".[24]

3.35 There is therefore strong anecdotal evidence that the incidence of trustee exemption clauses is widespread. Responses to the CP generally agreed that this was the case, and indicated that they considered the practice of including exemption provisions in trust instruments to be growing.

3.36 It is difficult to ascertain how often trustee exemption clauses are successfully relied on. Judicial statistics do not reveal the annual number of claims for breach of trust, let alone the number of disputes concerning trustee exemption clauses.

3.37 To date, there has only been a very limited number of reported English cases on trustee exemption clauses.[25] This figure should not be taken to indicate a small number of disputes involving trustee exemption clauses. The detail of trust litigation is commonly inaccessible, as it has historically often been held *in camera* or subject to reporting restrictions. In any case, many disputes concerning trustee exemption clauses will never reach court. The effect of all but one of the reported decisions was to uphold the efficacy of exemption provisions.[26] One might consequently expect potential claimant beneficiaries to be advised that, in the absence of trustee dishonesty, they have no basis on which to bring a claim. In such cases the complaint will not receive a public airing.

3.38 Several consultees also reported that in practice many claims which could be defeated by an exemption clause are settled. Trustees, they suggested, rarely take advantage of exemption clauses because to do so would destroy client relationships and could severely damage the trustee's reputation in the market. It is impossible to assess the veracity of this claim, but the comment emerged

---

[20] J Kessler QC, *Drafting Trusts and Will Trusts* (7th ed 2004) p 81.

[21] J Kessler QC, *Drafting Trusts and Will Trusts* (7th ed 2004) p 80.

[22] "This clause is for use in special cases": Prideaux, *Forms and Precedents in Conveyancing* (25th ed 1959) vol 3, p 158.

[23] *Butterworth's Encyclopaedia of Forms and Precedents* (5th ed 2001 Reissue) vol 40, p 512. The most recent edition provides that, "if, after full consideration with the settlor, an exemption clause is to be included, consideration should be given to its extent, and to whether a distinction is to be drawn between professional and lay trustees": *Butterworth's Encyclopaedia of Forms and Precedents* (5th ed 2005 Reissue) vol 40(1), p 158 (footnotes omitted).

[24] J Kessler QC, *Drafting Trusts and Will Trusts* (7th ed 2004) p 81.

[25] See Part 2.

[26] The exception was *Wight v Olswang (No 2)* (1999/2000) 2 ITELR 689: see para 2.21.

repeatedly throughout consultation and in Dr Dunn's research.[27] Of course, as reported cases show, even if many trustees elect not to rely on exemption clauses in practice, some clearly do use them to escape liability. The deterrent effect of the clauses may also mean that other claims are simply never brought. Nevertheless, if it is true that very few trustees actually rely on exemption clauses, the need for reform fades.

3.39 The extent of the problem is therefore far from clear. There is strong anecdotal evidence that the incidence of exemption clauses in trust instruments is widespread and growing. However, there are also suggestions that the extent of the problem is exaggerated and that in fact the number of trustees relying on blanket exemption clauses is relatively limited.

CONCLUSION

3.40 We remain of the view that, on balance, there is a problem that needs to be addressed. The strong anecdotal evidence that the creation of and reliance on trustee exemption clauses is widespread and growing supports this view. We are particularly concerned by the apparent inclusion of exemption provisions in trust instruments where the settlor does not fully understand their import.

3.41 We accept, however, that there are dangers in taking an over-simplified view of the role of trustee exemption clauses. As consultees made clear, any reform must take account of the desirability of retaining settlor autonomy and have regard to the possible adverse impact on beneficiaries and the wider consequences of regulation. It must also be proportionate to the mischief at which it is directed.

---

[27] See CP, paras 3.26 and 3.27.

PART 4
"PROFESSIONAL" AND "LAY": DISTINGUISHING BETWEEN DIFFERENT TYPES OF TRUSTEE

INTRODUCTION

4.1 The approach to trustee exemption clauses set out in the CP built upon a distinction between professional trustees and lay trustees.[1] In principle, the case for regulation of the former in their reliance upon exemption provisions was felt to be considerably stronger than the case for regulation of the latter. The CP accordingly asked whether consultees agreed that regulation should distinguish different types of trustee and, if so, whether the suggested categories of "professional" and "lay" trustees were the right ones.

4.2 These questions provoked much discussion amongst consultees. Arguments for and against the CP's provisional views made up a significant portion of the comments we received. We therefore report on this element of the consultation in some detail. However, it must be remembered that consultees' comments on this subject were made against the backdrop of the CP's provisional proposals for legislative regulation. Given our revised reform recommendations, we do not consider all the points raised, or follow through every argument to a conclusion.

SHOULD THERE BE A DISTINCTION BETWEEN DIFFERENT CLASSES OF TRUSTEE?

4.3 The CP considered that:

> … the case for regulation of the use of trustee exemption clauses by professional trustees is very strong, but that lay trustees should in general continue to be able to rely upon trustee exemption clauses. We provisionally propose therefore that any statutory regulation of such clauses should make a distinction, in broad terms, between professional trustees and lay trustees.[2]

4.4 The CP suggested that it is not proper that those providing professional trust services should be able to exclude themselves from all liability. Greater regulation of the reliance upon trustee exemption clauses by professional trustees, as opposed to lay trustees, was thought appropriate on the basis that most professional trustees:

(1) have (or hold themselves out as having) special skills and expertise;

(2) charge fees for their services; and

---

[1] CP, para 4.33 and following.

[2] CP, para 4.39.

(3)   have (or are in a better position than beneficiaries to obtain) insurance.[3]

4.5   The CP noted the expansion of liability for negligence on the part of many professional persons such as solicitors, barristers, accountants and financial advisers. It pointed out that trust law already makes a distinction between professional and lay trustees when defining their respective duties of care.[4]

Reaction on consultation

4.6   Most consultees agreed with the provisional view that there should be some distinction between different types of trustee.[5] Many supported the reasoning in the CP: professional trustees hold themselves out as having special knowledge, skill and expertise, and other professional persons do not exempt themselves from all liability in their everyday work.

4.7   A number of different arguments were raised by the minority who disagreed with the provisional proposal.

All trustees should be regulated

4.8   A number of consultees argued that regulation should extend to all categories of trustee.

4.9   One basis for this view was that it is unsatisfactory to allow any trustee to be relieved of the duty to act reasonably, as this undermines the purpose of the trust. Where lay trustees do not personally have the necessary skill or knowledge to fulfil their duty, they should seek advice from a suitably qualified person (at the expense of the trust fund) rather than be protected from their failure to take such advice.

4.10   Other consultees argued against the provisional proposal on the basis that professional trustees are already subject to harsher treatment than their lay colleagues. They pointed to the lower statutory and common law standard of care of lay trustees and the ability of lay trustees to take advantage of exculpatory relief[6] more easily than professionals. Any further differentiation would consequently be unnecessary and unfair. The higher standards expected of

---

[3]   The CP noted that professional trustees who already have professional negligence insurance pass on this cost in their fees. If such trustees are able to rely on an exemption clause the beneficiaries essentially pay for insurance from which they obtain no benefit. The real beneficiary of the exemption clause in these circumstances is the trustee's insurer. Lay trustees who do not charge are not (in the absence of express authorisation in the trust instrument) in a position to fund, and so generally do not take out, insurance.

[4]   Trustee Act 2000, s 1(1); *Bartlett v Barclays Bank Trust Co Ltd (Nos 1 & 2)* [1980] Ch 515.

[5]   We go on to consider whether the correct distinction is between "professional" and "lay" trustees. For the moment we continue to use to these terms to describe the two classes.

[6]   Trustee Act 1925, s 61 provides that "if it appears to the court that a trustee, whether appointed by the court or otherwise, is or may be personally liable for any breach of trust, whether the transaction alleged to be a breach of trust occurred before or after the commencement of this Act, but has acted honestly and reasonably, and ought fairly to be excused for the breach of trust and for omitting to obtain the directions of the court in the matter in which he committed such breach, then the court may relieve him either wholly or partly from personal liability for the same". The courts have been loath to extend this protection to professional trustees (see *Re Pauling's Settlement Trusts (No 1)* [1964] Ch 303, 338, per Willmer LJ).

professional trustees are illusory if exemption clauses allow professionals to operate "on a level playing field" with exempted lay trustees or even at a lower standard than lay trustees who do not have the benefit of exemption.

4.11 This, though, was a minority view. Other consultees saw good policy reasons why certain types of trustee should be able to continue to take advantage of trustee exemption clauses. As one response commented, "the duties of charitable trustees and others who hold positions of responsibility in the not-for-profit sector are already onerous enough and it would only serve to deter otherwise willing volunteers if they were held to be personally accountable to the same degree as someone who is professionally qualified and holds himself out as such".[7] Similar considerations could be considered to apply to those who accept gratuitous trusteeship on the basis of friendship or family ties.

4.12 We are not persuaded by consultees' arguments that all trustees should be regulated. Trustees would be open to criticism if they took advice on every issue of difficulty, as this would delay the administration of the trust as well as diminish the trust fund available for distribution to the beneficiaries. Accepting that trustees will only take advice selectively, there will be circumstances where trustees fail to recognise that advice should be sought or do not realise the dangers of their conduct.

Proposed two-class categorisation over-simplistic

4.13 A number of consultees suggested that the proposed division of trustees into two groups (professional and lay) fails to reflect the full range of trustees. They preferred a more sophisticated classification taking into account the skills and experience of the trustee and, in some cases, the settlor as counterparty.[8]

4.14 We are not convinced that these types of approach would improve our proposals; a clear message from consultation has been the need for clarity in any reform. The introduction of a more complicated test would not deliver this.

4.15 We are aware of the difficulties in distinguishing between different types of trustee and in correctly classifying the various types of trusteeship. It is true that a result of limiting ourselves to two categories is that both classes will include a broad variety of individuals and corporate entities. However, we are confident that, provided the definition is correctly framed, a simple distinction would be able adequately to classify the whole range of trustees for the purposes at hand.

Different treatment would cause difficulties where professional and lay trustees act together

4.16 A number of consultees suggested that the proposed distinction would give rise to problems where a trust has both professional and lay trustees. Trustees of

---

[7] Jonathan Cooke, Humphrey & Co.

[8] For example, the Association of Contentious Trusts and Probate Specialists preferred a three-fold categorisation: (1) Commercial Equals, where settlor and trustee are of equal sophistication and bargaining power; (2) Commercial Providers, who provide professional services for a fee to settlors of varying sophistication and power where the settlor and trustee cannot be presumed to be equal; and (3) Unpaid Trustees, who may or may not be professionals.

non-charitable trusts must act unanimously[9] and are jointly and severally liable for their acts and omissions.[10] If professional and lay trustees are subject to different levels of regulation, the lay members of a trustee board may be able to rely on an exemption clause to escape liability in respect of a collective decision whereas the professionals will not. This, consultees argued, is unfair and could hinder trust administration where a professional trustee wishing to proceed cautiously acts (or is asked to act) with a lay trustee willing to take risks.

4.17   We are not persuaded by this argument. As previously discussed, professional and lay trustees are already subject to different standards of care. Beneficiaries are consequently already able to hold professionals liable for unanimously made decisions where lay co-trustees are not liable. Professional trustees are also likely to have the "deepest pockets" (or be covered by insurance) and so in any case will be the probable first port of call for any claimant.

HOW TO DISTINGUISH PROFESSIONAL AND LAY TRUSTEES

4.18   The CP provisionally proposed that:

> … any distinction between lay trustees and professional trustees be made on the basis [of the existing legislative definitions contained in section 28 of the Trustee Act 2000].[11]

4.19   Section 28 distinguishes trustees "acting in a professional capacity" from those not so acting in order to establish a statutory entitlement to remuneration. Subsection (5) provides that a trustee "acts in a professional capacity" if he:

> … acts in the course of a profession or business which consists of or includes the provision of services in connection with –
>
> (a) the management or administration of trusts generally or a particular kind of trust, or
>
> (b) any particular aspect of the management or administration of trusts generally or a particular kind of trust,
>
> and the services he provides to or on behalf of the trust fall within that description.

4.20   The CP favoured the section 28 approach over the Trust Law Committee's proposal that regulation should apply to any "trustee remunerated for his services

---

[9]   *Luke v South Kensington Hotel Co* (1879) LR 11 Ch D 121; *Re Dixon* (1826) 2 GL & J 114; *Re Flower and Metropolitan Board of Works* (1884) 27 Ch D 592.

[10]   See Sir John Leach MR in *Wilson v Moore* (1833) 1 My & K 126; *Edwards v Hood-Barrs* [1905] 1 Ch 20.

[11]   CP, para 4.39.

as trustee".[12] It considered that a test based on remuneration would allow canny trustees to avoid regulation by declining direct payment in favour of more indirect benefits.[13] It also preferred the section 28 definition on grounds of consistency.

The reaction on consultation

4.21   There was only very limited support for the provisional proposal. Some consultees agreed with the CP's argument regarding consistency with the Trustee Act 2000. Others shared the CP's doubts about the alternative distinction between remunerated and unremunerated trustees.

4.22   A significant majority of consultees objected to the CP's proposed test. Many drew attention to the fundamental difference between the purpose of the definition in the Trustee Act and its intended use in relation to trustee exemption clauses. Section 28 was drafted as an enabling provision (to define the circumstances in which trustees are entitled to remuneration) whereas in the context of trustee exemption the definition would be used as a restrictive provision (to deny certain trustees the right to invoke exemption clauses). As a consequence of its original purpose, the section 28 definition is widely drawn, enabling a broad spectrum of trustees to qualify as professional and hence to become entitled to claim remuneration.

4.23   We accept the criticisms made of the provisional proposal in this respect. On reflection, we concede that section 28 of the Trustee Act 2000 does not provide an appropriate distinction between those who should be subject to regulation in relation to trustee exemption clauses and those who should not. We accept that while consistency of definition may be desirable, the context in which a definition is drawn is likely to influence its scope and extent.

4.24   We now believe that it is important to ensure that trustees who may be professional persons are not regulated in relation to exemption clauses where they have been acting as trustees pro bono. Many trusts are heavily reliant for their efficient operation and management on the participation of skilled professionals who do not charge for their services.

4.25   This is particularly an issue for charities where professionals accept gratuitous appointment for altruistic reasons. Given that such trustees add to the quality of decision-making, while helping to reduce the cost of (external) professional services, there are strong policy reasons for encouraging their contribution. We recognise that the prospect of the imposition of onerous obligations without the security and comfort of a trustee exemption clause could lead to a decrease in the numbers of much-needed experts willing to accept trusteeship without

---

[12]   But "not an executor-trustee who received a legacy as a token of the testator's affection or esteem, being of a significant lesser value than the amount of remuneration that might reasonably be expected to be paid for the services as executor-trustee". See Trust Law Committee, *Consultation Paper: Trustee Exemption Clauses* (June 1999) para 7.7. A similar test was supported by the New Zealand Law Commission: Some Problems in the Law of Trusts (2002) New Zealand Law Commission Report No 79, para 14.

[13]   See CP, para 4.39.

reward. This would go against our initial objective of encouraging trustees to act without expectation or receipt of remuneration.[14]

4.26 On reflection, we consider that a more appropriate and transparent distinction would be one based on the trustee's receipt of remuneration: in short whether the trustee is paid or unpaid.

4.27 The CP's main argument against a remuneration test was that it might be avoided by (or even give rise to) practices whereby a person receives no payment for acting as trustee but other services are charged for.[15] Although several consultees confirmed that such practices exist,[16] a significant number did not consider this to be a sufficiently good reason to resist a remuneration test. Some considered the CP's concerns to be unjustified as professional codes of conduct and ethics bar such activities and because any trustee acting in this way would also be in breach of fiduciary duty. Others argued that the objection could be readily overcome by a wide definition of remuneration, whereby indirect as well as direct benefits are taken into account.[17]

4.28 We consider the issue of avoidance via indirect payments when considering our recommended rule of practice at paragraph 6.65.

Conclusion

4.29 We are now convinced that the correct approach is to distinguish between professional and lay trustees solely on the basis of remuneration. Such a test would, we accept, better capture the type of trustee who should be subject to trustee exemption clause regulation. The test would be readily comprehensible, certain and, in the vast majority of cases, of easy application.

4.30 We do not comment further here on precisely how the concept of remuneration should be framed. The detailed definition (in particular, the extent to which it is necessary to address the dangers of avoidance) will depend on the regulatory system in which it has to operate.

---

[14] CP, para 4.16.

[15] CP, para 4.39.

[16] Examples given include accountants accepting gratuitous trusteeship but charging for trust accounting, banks accepting gratuitous trusteeship and charging for portfolio management and firms of solicitors not charging for the provision of a trustee, but receiving a fee for trust administration and advice.

[17] For example, by defining remuneration in terms of direct and indirect financial benefit to the trustee or an associated person consequent on acting as trustee.

PART 5
STATUTORY REGULATION OF TRUSTEE EXEMPTION CLAUSES: THE CP'S PROVISIONAL PROPOSALS FOR REFORM

INTRODUCTION

5.1 The CP considered a range of possible models of statutory regulation of trustee exemption clauses. It provisionally rejected a number of alternatives and sought the views of consultees.

5.2 In Appendix A, we report briefly on consultees' views of the options provisionally rejected in the CP. With due respect to those who argued in favour of these regulatory approaches, we do not attempt a comprehensive analysis of every option. Consultation confirmed our provisional view that none of the alternatives rejected in the CP offers an appropriate model for reform, in most cases on the grounds set out in the CP.

THE CP'S PROVISIONALLY PROPOSED SCHEME

5.3 The CP made three provisional proposals which encapsulated the tenor of its preferred scheme.

5.4 The CP's principal provisional proposal was that statute should restrict the effectiveness of clauses where the conduct of the trustee crosses the threshold of negligence. As we put it:

> … a professional trustee should not be able to rely on any provision in a trust instrument excluding liability for breach of trust arising from negligence.[1]

5.5 In order to obviate avoidance of regulation by the use of duty exclusion clauses or extended powers clauses, we made an ancillary provisional proposal to the effect that the court could disapply such clauses:

> … where reliance on such clauses would be inconsistent with the overall purposes of the trust and it would be unreasonable in the circumstances for the trustee to be exempted from liability.[2]

5.6 At the same time, we attempted to offer a degree of greater protection to trustees (both professional and lay) by means of a further provisional proposal:

> … that all trustees should be given power to make payments out of the trust fund to purchase indemnity insurance to cover their liability for breach of trust.[3]

---

[1] CP, para 4.85. We refer to this as the CP's "primary reform proposal".

[2] CP, para 4.97.

[3] CP, para 4.32.

5.7 It is possible to dispense with this further provisional proposal in short order. We have concluded on the basis of consultation responses that it is not appropriate to recommend such a power. A detailed discussion of consultees' reactions to the provisional proposal and our reasons for abandoning this policy suggestion are set out in Appendix B.

5.8 In the remainder of this Part we re-evaluate in light of the consultation process the CP's central provisional proposals relating to (1) liability for negligence, and (2) anti-avoidance.

NO RELIANCE ON CLAUSES WHERE A PROFESSIONAL TRUSTEE IS NEGLIGENT

5.9 The CP outlined a number of reasons for its view that trustees should be prohibited from excluding liability for simple (rather than gross) negligence.[4] It noted that negligence is the most common cause of loss to trust funds and highlighted the expansion of professional liability for negligence in many areas. These factors, it argued, make it logical and consistent to deny professional trustees resort to exemption clauses when their conduct can be characterised as negligent. The CP's provisional proposal in this respect matched that of the Trust Law Committee ("TLC") consultation paper, which also advocated negligence rather than gross negligence as the appropriate threshold for legislative regulation.[5]

5.10 A clear majority of consultees agreed that the general approach to legislative regulation set out in the CP's primary reform proposal was preferable to the CP's alternative reform options. Responses put forward three main arguments in support of the primary reform proposal. First, it is appropriate for professional trustees to conform to professional standards of care, and the most natural professional standard is to act in a manner that is not negligent. Secondly, professional trustees are able to protect themselves against the consequences of liability for negligence by indemnity insurance. Thirdly, this proposed approach to the regulation of exemption clauses would provide more certainty than other options discussed in the CP.

5.11 However, significant reservations emerged. These concerns (expressed in written consultation responses, in published articles on the consultation paper and in open meetings during the consultation period) were not restricted to those who expressly opposed the primary reform proposal. Some were raised by those who appeared otherwise to favour the CP's scheme, and so must be taken into account in considering the apparent level of support for legislative reform.

Adverse consequences

5.12 The principal concern expressed during the consultation process relates to the likely adverse effects of any regulation along the lines proposed by the CP. Many of the arguments about regulatory impact raised by consultees are specific to particular types of trust (for example, commercial trusts). We do not consider

---

[4] See further Appendix A, para A.43.

[5] Trust Law Committee, *Consultation Paper: Trustee Exemption Clauses* (June 1999) para 7.7.

these distinct concerns in this Part but discuss them in some detail in Appendix C.

5.13 The CP raised the issue of the regulatory impact of its provisional proposals, acknowledging that "the regulation of trustee exemption clauses may have a considerable impact on the use of trusts and that any reform of the law must take account of the potential economic implications".[6] Its efforts to assess the likely consequences of reform were founded on the socio-economic research set out in Part III of the paper. Further, it invited consultees to provide information or views on the economic implications and the regulatory impact of reform.[7]

5.14 A general thrust of consultation was that, notwithstanding its efforts to do so, the CP had failed to take adequate account of the likely adverse consequences of legislative regulation. Many respondents were clear that whether or not one agreed with the principled arguments in favour of reform, regulation along the lines provisionally proposed in the CP would come at a great practical cost.

5.15 Not all of the concerns about the effects of regulation were directed specifically at the CP's favoured means of regulation; many consultees raised the practical consequences of reform in response to the larger question of whether there should be reform at all. Nevertheless, virtually all of the adverse impacts suggested by consultees apply as much to the CP's primary reform proposal as to any other forms of statutory regulation that would restrict reliance on trustee exemption clauses.

Cost and availability of indemnity insurance

5.16 Some responses raised indemnity insurance as a particular concern when warning of the potential impact of regulation. As Appendix B describes, a significant number of consultees believed that the effect of restricting reliance on trustee exemption clauses would be to drive up indemnity insurance premiums, possibly to prohibitive levels. It was argued that in some circumstances insurance might even become unavailable. The cost and availability of insurance could disproportionately affect smaller paid trustees, and thereby reduce the quality of those left operating in the market.

5.17 These concerns were mirrored in Dr Dunn's socio-economic research.[8] It is therefore difficult to dismiss the risk that regulation could cause significant premium increases and possibly the unavailability of indemnity insurance.

5.18 In addition to being a significant issue in its own right, the future availability of affordable indemnity insurance has a knock-on effect on the other potential consequences of regulation discussed below. The CP never suggested that trustee indemnity insurance would be a viable alternative to the protection offered by exemption clauses. Nevertheless, the provisional proposals for the promotion of insurance and the regulation of trustee exemption clauses were clearly connected. The fact that affordable trustee indemnity insurance might, as a

---

[6] CP, para 1.13.

[7] CP, para 5.16.

[8] See CP, para 3.82 and following.

consequence of regulation, become unavailable to some trustees significantly increases the impact of the other risks of regulation.

Reluctance to accept trusteeship

5.19   A number of consultees suggested that any legislative restriction on the ability to rely on trustee exemption clauses would be bound to deter potential trustees from accepting appointment. Those who took this line argued that it is in no-one's interests for trusts to suffer for the want of trustees. Dr Dunn's socio-economic research reached a similar conclusion, indicating a widespread belief that regulation of trustee exemption clauses would affect the take-up of trusteeship.[9]

5.20   While we understand consultees' concerns, we are not convinced that regulation would necessarily give rise to significant problems of this kind. The CP was clear that its provisional proposals should not apply to lay trustees and we have explained that we now think only paid trustees should be subject to regulation. Paid trustees have a commercial incentive to continue to act and would be unlikely to turn down business lightly.

5.21   Nevertheless, we accept that there must be some risk that regulation of the type proposed in the CP could cause a reduction in the number of available trustees and could make it more difficult for "higher-risk" trusts to find a trustee at all.

Transfer of trusteeship to other jurisdictions

5.22   Dr Dunn's socio-economic research suggested that many trustees believe that regulation could lead to the transfer of trusts to jurisdictions which do not restrict reliance on trustee exemption clauses. The CP argued that this was not a real risk on the grounds that other factors (the settlor's location and taxation) are more important than regulation to a settlor selecting the jurisdiction of a trust. In addition, the most convenient alternative jurisdictions already regulate trustee exemption clauses and so there is little incentive to relocate there.

5.23   Nothing in consultation has led us to change our overall view that legislative regulation would be unlikely to promote a mass migration of trusteeship overseas. However, we do accept that there is a danger that this jurisdiction could lose certain trust business – notably in the financial markets – were the overall package of regulation provisionally proposed in the CP to be implemented.

Defensive trusteeship

5.24   A number of consultees suggested that the removal of the protection of exemption clauses would be likely to change trustee behaviour. Trustees denied the comfort of an exemption clause would, they argued, be likely to act defensively. Whereas currently trustees might be willing to take risks that they considered to be in the beneficiaries' interests, once regulated they would only

---

[9]   Nearly two thirds of trustee respondents to the survey predicted that prohibition of reliance on trustee exemption clauses would cause the number of people choosing to accept trusteeship to decrease (CP, para 3.44).

act where they were sure there was no chance of liability. Some trustees might become reluctant to accept or exercise discretionary powers at all.[10]

5.25   Many consultees also thought that the type of regulation provisionally proposed in the CP would slow down trustee decision-making. Trustees would refuse to act without lengthy discussions and in many cases legal advice. Delays in trust administration would be common. Trustees would become less responsive to beneficiaries' requests.

5.26   Any increase in defensive trusteeship would, it was argued, result in increased operational costs. Costs would rise as trustees tightened their compliance systems, held longer and more frequent meetings and spent more time ensuring that there was written evidence of the diligent carrying out of their duties. The trust fund would be likely to bear the cost of the increased use of professional advisers.

5.27   On balance, we accept that there is a risk that concerns about potential liability would impact on the way trustees conduct trust business. This might not in all respects be a bad thing: it will not always be in the overall interests of beneficiaries for trustees to be able to act quickly and cheaply if in doing so they act negligently. However, it is also true that less flexible trusteeship, increased legal costs and slower trustee decision-making would be unwelcome developments. Most beneficiaries would agree that the best trustees are prepared to act decisively and expeditiously in order to serve the beneficiaries' interests.

Increase in litigation

5.28   Many consultees believed that prohibiting reliance on trustee exemption clauses would cause a rise in trust litigation. This could of course be said to be an inevitable corollary of reform, in that where beneficiaries are currently barred from proceeding against a negligent trustee by reason of an exemption clause, regulation would enable them to bring the trustee to account.

5.29   Litigation is, however, in more general terms undesirable. An increase in trust litigation would have a deleterious effect on trust funds which would be dissipated by legal costs. Any growth of a "compensation culture" among beneficiaries could lead to unmeritorious yet time-consuming claims[11] and so deter people from accepting appointment as trustee.

5.30   Trustees are already, in some respects, particularly vulnerable to litigation. Trusteeship is based upon sophisticated concepts and is subject to complex, often impenetrable, areas of the law. It may well involve difficult human or business circumstances. In many cases, trustees are required to take decisions which will inevitably be resented by one or more parties. Consequently, it is

---

[10]   One respondent pointed to the position in the United States, where many trustees refuse to accept discretionary powers in trust deeds on the basis that there is too much risk in operating them. If alternatively the powers remained but trustees became reluctant to use them, it would be difficult for beneficiaries to establish a breach of trust based solely on a trustee's refusal to exercise a discretionary power.

[11]   Which might be compromised by trustees anxious to protect their reputation.

sometimes very difficult for trustees to avoid acting in a way that is susceptible to challenge by the beneficiaries.

5.31 It is impossible to predict exactly how trust litigation would be affected by the CP's proposed regulation of trustee exemption clauses. However, we agree with consultees that it is inevitable that the regulation of trustee exemption clauses would lead to an increase in litigation, as claims that were previously unavailable to beneficiaries would become tenable. While in many cases we think that this would produce a justifiable result – the protection of the trust fund – we accept that in others the overall effect would be negative.

Assessment of consultees' concerns

5.32 It is claimed that the risks associated with statutory reform along the lines provisionally proposed in the CP have the potential to be hugely damaging to the trust industry. We are aware that many of those who predict such disastrous consequences have a personal interest in avoiding regulation and that the likelihood of the projected adverse effects arising has not been conclusively evidenced.

5.33 It may be that the effects of statutory intervention of the sort envisaged by the CP would not be as problematic as some consultees suggested. The Unfair Contract Terms Act 1977 has operated to prohibit reliance on contractual terms excluding or limiting liability for nearly 30 years and, although some operators may find its provisions inconvenient, markets have adapted to those restrictions.[12] However, we accept that the concerns raised by consultees are more likely to be well-founded in the trusts context. In particular, the ongoing nature of the trust relationship, the onerous "default" duties on trustees and the position of successor trustees who assume office long after the original settlement augment the potential for damaging consequences.

5.34 The cost implications of the CP's provisional reform proposals are difficult to quantify. We have already commented upon the problems in obtaining evidence of the current incidence and extent of trustee negligence, trustee reliance on exemption clauses and beneficiary loss.[13] Without reliable data we are not in a position to assess properly the likely impact of regulation on the cost of providing trust services. Any putative regulatory measure of the kind put forward in the CP clearly has the potential to raise costs. In the absence of evidence to the contrary, we have to accept that there is a danger that cost increases would be significant.

5.35 We also cannot be certain whether such increases in operating costs would be absorbed by trustees or born by beneficiaries via price increases. A determination of the likely outcome would require reliable economic estimates of

---

[12] It is interesting to note that the Law Commission's 1969 report on exemption clauses in contracts which lay behind the enactment of the Unfair Contract Terms Act 1977 reported similar concerns amongst consultees: "It was feared that a general reasonableness test would create an intolerable degree of uncertainty in commercial affairs, lead to an increased amount of litigation, and make it difficult for legal advisers satisfactorily to advise their clients" (Exemption Clauses in Contracts First Report: Amendments to the Sale of Goods Act 1893 (1969) Law Com No 24; Scot Law Com No 12, para 103).

[13] See paras 3.28 and following.

elasticity of supply and demand in both the trust and insurance industries, from which to calculate the probable effect on prices and outputs. Such information is not available.

5.36 The potential non-economic consequences of the CP's provisionally proposed regulation are even more difficult to predict and their assessment must largely be a matter of judgement. We accept the concerns of many respected consultees that the scheme provisionally proposed in the CP might adversely affect the behaviour of trustees and the flexibility of the trust device.

5.37 Whereas it is impossible to be certain whether any cost increases would ultimately impact on trustees or on trust funds, such non-economic consequences would be largely borne by beneficiaries rather than trustees. Beneficiaries would be affected by defensive trusteeship and delays in the exercise of powers and discretions. Settlors and beneficiaries would be denied the benefits of flexible trusts and would face the consequences of any fall-off in the numbers of those willing to act as trustee.

ANTI-AVOIDANCE

5.38 "Trustee exemption clause" is a generic term describing clauses which exempt trustees from liability. Within that over-arching category there are a number of specific types of provision, all of which operate in technically distinct ways.

5.39 The CP's primary reform proposal focused on clauses which purport to limit or exclude the trustee's liability for acts that would otherwise be actionable. For example, "no trustee shall be liable for any loss to the trust fund unless that loss was caused by his own actual fraud". Such clauses can be described as "liability exclusion" clauses.

5.40 Liability exclusion clauses are not the only means by which trustees can obtain protection from liability for breach of trust. If these alternative means were not brought within the scope of legislation they would offer loopholes by which trustees could escape the effects of regulation. The CP consequently made an ancillary provisional proposal as an anti-avoidance measure.[14]

5.41 The CP referred to three types of clause: trustee indemnity clauses, extended powers clauses and duty modification clauses.[15] Consultees also discussed the possible application of clauses limiting the quantum of liability. First, we briefly consider indemnity clauses and "liability-capping" clauses before turning to the most difficult categories of provision – duty modification and extended powers clauses.

Indemnity clauses

5.42 An indemnity clause is a provision in the trust instrument entitling the trustee to indemnity from the trust fund in respect of any liability arising for breach of trust. The CP argued that to the extent that trustee exemption clauses are regulated it

---

[14] See para 5.5.

[15] The CP referred to the latter as "duty exclusion clauses". For the purposes of this Report, we use the somewhat broader term. Duty modification and duty exclusion clauses are also known as "ouster clauses".

must follow that trustees should not be able to obtain recompense from the trust fund in respect of their liabilities.

5.43 Consultees were almost unanimous in their agreement with our provisional view. To permit a trustee to claim indemnity from the trust fund would mean that, although the trustee had been liable to the trust for a breach of trust, the trust fund rather than the trustee would suffer the loss caused by the breach. Such a result would be absurd.

Clauses limiting the quantum of liability

5.44 A number of consultees commented on another type of clause not addressed in the CP – clauses in trust instruments which purport to limit or cap the quantum of trustees' liability. Consultees suggested that some trustees negotiate clauses that place a ceiling on their liability. Examples given involved limiting the trustee's liability to a specified figure (for example, £1m), to the value of the trust fund at the time of the alleged negligence, or to a multiple of (for example, 20 times) the annual administration fee. Alternatively, liability could be limited to foreseeable or immediate loss rather than full consequential loss, or to an amount equivalent to a reasonable level of insurance. Some consultees argued that liability-capping could soften the effects of regulating paid trustees, as trustees would have a definite "down-side" (a maximum amount of liability) to weigh up against a known "up-side" (their fees).

5.45 While liability-capping may be a useful and appropriate means of sharing the risk of trustee negligence, we doubt the feasibility of formulating regulation around such clauses. There would obviously have to be some restriction on the level of the cap; otherwise there would be nothing to stop it being set at £1. Legislation allowing liability-capping to the extent it is "reasonable"[16] would not provide the certainty required by trustees and insurers. We are not convinced by the suggestion that liability could be limited to the amount of insurance available. Such an approach would leave trustees with no incentive to push insurers for competitive quotes for comprehensive cover. It would also leave the protection of the trust fund vulnerable to variances in insurance cover resulting from the trustees' general claims record.

Duty modification and extended powers clauses

5.46 Some of the most difficult issues underlying the trustee exemption clauses project concern the treatment of duty modification and extended powers clauses. As a result of this complexity, it is necessary to deal with both types of clause in some detail. In this section we restate the approach to duty modification and extended powers clauses provisionally proposed in the CP and outline consultees' reaction to that suggested treatment. We then explore the suggestion that regulation could distinguish between different sorts of duty modification provision.

5.47 A duty modification clause modifies or excludes one or more of the underlying duties to which a trustee would otherwise be subject as a matter of law.[17] By

---

[16] This is the position under the Unfair Contract Terms Act 1977, s 11(4).

[17] For example, "the trustees shall be under no duty to diversify the investment of the trust fund".

modifying duties, such clauses make it less likely that a breach of duty will be committed by a trustee, and therefore that a beneficiary may make a claim. An extended powers clause operates by defining the powers exercisable by the trustee more widely than those usually enjoyed as a matter of law.[18] The clause thereby confers upon the trustee greater latitude than would be normally expected, with the result that it is less likely that the trustee will act *ultra vires*.

5.48 Narrow definitions of duty and wide definitions of powers both therefore have the potential to make it considerably more difficult for a beneficiary to establish that a trustee has committed a breach of trust (whether by breach of duty, or by acting *ultra vires*). Clauses of this kind can therefore be employed by trustees in an attempt to undermine regulation of clauses expressly excluding liability.

The CP

5.49 The CP introduced the questions posed by duty modification and extended powers clauses by examining the analysis of the TLC in its consultation paper.[19] The TLC recognised both the utility of these clauses in certain trust situations and their relevance to liability exclusion.

5.50 In an attempt to minimise any restrictions on the autonomy of the settlor, the TLC investigated the possibility of applying different treatment to different types of duty modification clauses. They considered the viability of regulating only those clauses which purported (wholly or partly) to "negative a positive duty that would otherwise lie on the trustee".[20] Clauses excluding a negative duty[21] would not be subject to regulation. The regulation of clauses negativing a positive duty alone would, they thought, be sufficient to protect the regulation of liability exclusion clauses as:

> … the effect…would be to permit something to be done which would otherwise automatically be a breach of trust, and it will still have to be judged whether it was indeed an appropriate exercise of such power in all the circumstances for the trustee to do what is being considered. In other words, a power to do a thing is not a power to do it badly. If it is done badly, then there will be liability for breach of trust.[22]

5.51 Ultimately, however, the TLC was unable to overcome the difficulties of distinguishing between positive and negative duties as in many cases duties can

---

[18] For example, "the trustees may pay taxes and other expenses out of income although they would otherwise be paid out of capital".

[19] See CP, para 4.90 and following.

[20] Trust Law Committee, *Consultation Paper: Trustee Exemption Clauses* (June 1999) para 7.11. By "a positive duty" the TLC meant a duty to do something. The paper gives the example of a duty to supervise a company in which a trust has a shareholding. This would be negatived by a clause providing that the trustee is under no duty to supervise the company.

[21] The Trust Law Committee consultation paper gives the example of a clause modifying the duty (now superseded) not to invest other than as authorised by the Trustee Investment Act 1961 by granting an express power to invest in "quadratic bonds": Trust Law Committee, *Consultation Paper: Trustee Exemption Clauses* (June 1999) para 7.13.

[22] Trust Law Committee, *Consultation Paper: Trustee Exemption Clauses* (June 1999) para 7.13.

be framed in either positive or negative terms.[23] Without a clear distinction between the two classes of provision, it would be impossible to give any meaningful legislative effect to their tentative approach.

5.52 The CP agreed with the TLC's view that some types of duty modification clause do not, as a matter of construction, protect the trustee. It took this argument further, and suggested that where the trust instrument negates a positive duty that trustees would otherwise have, the trustees may not be protected if they act negligently. If the trustees retain the power to follow the course of action they would otherwise have been bound to follow, they may be liable if they negligently fail to exercise the power. [24]

5.53 However, the CP recognised that not all duty modification clauses can be interpreted in this way. It would be possible to draw up a duty modification clause providing that "the trustee shall not be obliged to take reasonable care in the conduct of the affairs of the trust". We use the term "general standard of care modification clause" to describe such provisions which purport to modify the underlying duty of care owed by trustees. The effect of such a provision would be to exclude entirely the trustee's duty to act in a non-negligent manner with the result that any negligent action or omission could not constitute a breach of trust. Provided that the clause did not seek to authorise the trustee to act dishonestly or in bad faith, it would not be susceptible to attack on the grounds set out in *Armitage v Nurse*.[25]

5.54 The CP commented that extended powers clauses may also fail to protect the trustees on their true construction. The fact that an extended powers clause authorises a particular act does not mean that the trustees cannot be challenged for carrying out that act. Trustees are required to act with care and prudence, and a failure to do so will result in liability for breach of trust, irrespective of whether the act complained of is within the scope of any power. The CP nevertheless identified certain extended powers clauses as a cause for concern, and proposed that extended powers clauses should be subject to the same regulation as duty modification clauses.

5.55 The CP was therefore clear that some regulation of duty modification and extended powers clauses was essential if the primary reform proposal was to function meaningfully. However, it faced a problem. Duty modification and extended powers clauses are often included in trust instruments for perfectly good and practical reasons not motivated by an intention to avoid liability for breach of trust. The CP recognised that "the trust is in essence a flexible device, and it should be open to settlors to restrict the scope of the duties owed by trustees in particular cases and to confer very wide powers on them".[26]

---

[23] The Trust Law Committee consultation paper gives the example of a duty to take reasonable care to preserve the trust property which can be rephrased as a duty not to be negligent: Trust Law Committee, *Consultation Paper: Trustee Exemption Clauses* (June 1999) para 7.14.

[24] See CP, para 4.91 and following for discussion.

[25] [1998] Ch 241.

[26] CP, para 4.89.

5.56 The CP accordingly took the view that duty modification and extended powers clauses should not be prohibited as a matter of course, and that regulatory control of such clauses would have to be "sophisticated and responsive to the particular circumstances of each case".[27] It provisionally proposed that the court should have the power to strike down duty modification clauses and extended powers clauses which are excessively wide in circumstances where trustees are abusing their fiduciary position:

> ... in determining whether professional trustees have been negligent, the court should have the power to disapply duty exclusion clauses or extended powers clauses where reliance on such clauses would be inconsistent with the overall purposes of the trust and it would be unreasonable in the circumstances for the trustee to be exempted from liability.[28]

Reaction on consultation

5.57 Many consultees supported the CP's provisional proposal. Most did so on the basis that failure to regulate duty modification clauses and extended powers clauses would lead to the circumvention of the proposed regulation of liability exclusion provisions. It was, in other words, a necessary anti-avoidance measure.

5.58 Respondents also agreed with the CP's comments about the importance of modifying clauses. Law Debenture Trust Corporation Plc summarised the positive role played by such clauses by outlining three types of common application:

   (1)   to permit the trust to operate in the manner intended by the parties to the transaction;

   (2)   to ensure that the trustee's role is that which the parties intend it to be; and

   (3)   to ensure that the trustee's role can be undertaken at a cost which those parties are willing to bear.

5.59 Consultees gave numerous examples of clauses which are necessary and appropriate in the particular circumstances, such as:

PRIVATE TRUSTS

   (1)   when apportioning trust receipts between income and capital beneficiaries, the trustee is under no duty to consider the interests of the remaindermen;

   (2)   when the trustee is not obliged to monitor what directors are doing where a substantial majority of the shares in a company is owned by the trustee;

---

[27]   CP, para 4.95.

[28]   CP, para 4.97.

COMMERCIAL TRUSTS

    (3)   in unsecured bond issues, when trustees who have received a certificate confirming that no event of default has occurred are entitled to assume (unless they have actual notice to the contrary) that no such event has in fact occurred;

    (4)   in security transactions, when trustees are not obliged independently to investigate title to the charged assets; and

    (5)   in securitisation transactions, when trustees are not required to monitor or supervise the activities of an administrator or servicer.

5.60   Respondents therefore largely agreed with the CP's analysis of the need to address duty modification and extended powers clauses, and the need to protect the continued use of such clauses so as to permit the proper demarcation of the role of the trustee.

5.61   However, many respondents strongly opposed the CP's suggested means of balancing these needs. There was widespread disquiet that the effect of permitting the court to disapply duty modification and extended powers clauses would be to create damaging uncertainty about reliance on such clauses and so prejudice their proper use.

5.62   Consultees' complaints of uncertainty were pitched at two levels:

    (1)   that if the court were given discretion to disapply particular types of clause in trust instruments, trustees would not know whether actions taken in accordance with the terms of the trust might subsequently be subject to challenge; and

    (2)   that the terms of the discretion as provisionally proposed were themselves insufficiently clear and would prove difficult if not impossible to apply.

UNCERTAINTY AS TO RELIANCE ON THE TERMS OF THE TRUST

5.63   The strongest concern of those who objected to the provisional proposal was that the effect of denying trustees automatic reliance on clauses purporting to modify their duties would be to undermine certainty in the apparent terms of the trust instrument.

5.64   Respondents pointed to the basic need of all trustees to be sure of the terms of their trust. Legislation which cast uncertainty on these terms would lead to instability. Legal advisers would be unable to predict at the outset whether or not a particular clause would be disapplied in the event of a future claim. Trustees in the course of their trust administration would not be sure whether an act or omission which appeared to be in accordance with the terms of the trust instrument could lead to liability for breach of trust. No matter how careful the trustees were, there would be a risk of the court disapplying the clause purporting to authorise the trustees' action or omission at some point in the future.

5.65   The CP recognised that its provisional proposal would introduce some uncertainty, but did not consider this to be excessive or unjustifiable. It commented that "an element of uncertainty is inevitable wherever the court is called upon to examine the conduct of individuals, in this case trustees, after the event, in any attempt to discern whether they have been negligent".[29]

5.66 The comments of consultees suggest that the proposed test would cause damage whether or not matters actually ended up in court. The mere possibility of challenge would be enough to destroy the utility of the clause, and in some cases undermine the viability of the whole trust.[30] It may well be that in such circumstances the relevant clauses, if attacked, would be held by a court to be wholly reasonable. However, the inability to rely on the clause without the possibility of future challenge could in some circumstances be enough to deter trustees from acting or settlors from using a trust.

5.67 Consultees thought that the consequences would be particularly damaging in the context of commercial trusts. They argued that the effectiveness of such trusts rests on all the parties being clear as to their respective rights, powers and obligations. Current law and practice governing the use of duty exclusion and extended powers clauses allow issuers, investors and trustees to be certain of their position.[31] To introduce a test along the lines proposed in the CP would destroy this certainty.

5.68 Similar problems would arise in relation to standard form private trusts which are mass-marketed by companies providing trust services. Companies marketing such trusts need to be sure of the obligations the trusts would impose from the outset. They will usually require a barrister's "clean" opinion. It would, they suggested, be unsatisfactory if that opinion had to refer to the fact that the court might prevent the trustee relying on a particular clause if it thought it unreasonable in all the circumstances.

5.69 Consultees also emphasised the importance of duty modification and extended powers clauses to trusts of "difficult" assets or beneficiaries.[32] It is often fundamental to the operation of such trusts that the trustees are not required to take certain actions or make decisions that would normally be expected of trustees. The protection offered by such clauses is often a pre-requisite of the trustees' willingness to act.

5.70 Consultees warned that the CP's proposed anti-avoidance measure would also diminish the flexibility inherent in the trust concept. Settlors would continue to be able to shape the role of trustee so as to match their intentions by the inclusion of duty modification clauses in the trust instrument. However, such clauses would not be conclusive. Faced with the possibility of future challenge, trustees would in many cases refuse to rely on such terms. They might even argue against the inclusion of the terms in the trust instrument in the first place. As a result, the role of trustee could revert to the fulfilment of the default powers and duties

---

[29] CP, para 4.96.

[30] Compare consultees' objections to a test of reasonableness for exemption clauses generally, Appendix A, paras A.16 to A.17.

[31] See Financial Markets Law Committee, *Trustee Exemption Clauses Report – Issue 62* (May 2004) p 5.

[32] See para 3.13.

established by equity. The flexibility to mould that role to particular circumstances would, to a greater or lesser extent, be diminished.

5.71 Some consultees suggested that the terms of the proposed test would themselves give rise to uncertainty. The concepts of "reliance on such clauses being inconsistent with the overall purposes of the trust" and exemption being "unreasonable in the circumstances" were criticised as ambiguous and difficult to apply in practice. Consultees suggested that such difficulties would be particularly pronounced in the short-term as there would be no guiding body of case law. However, case law could not wholly resolve the ambiguity of the test, as judicial decisions on the test's application would usually be confined to their own facts.

5.72 The phrase "the overall purposes of the trust" was subject to particular criticism. Consultees suggested that this would introduce a new concept into trust law. They questioned how a court would determine the purpose of a trust other than by its provisions, including any duty modification clauses.

Assessment of consultees' concerns

5.73 It is clear that any attempt to regulate duty modification and extended powers clauses in trusts has the potential to do harm. Such clauses are a key feature of trust practice and an important aspect of the trust's much-valued flexibility.

5.74 We therefore accept the validity of the arguments against the provisional approach set out in the CP. We acknowledge that the attempt we made to block the loophole presented by duty modification and extended powers clauses could create disproportionate problems of the sort outlined by consultees. What, then, are the alternatives?

NO REGULATION OF DUTY MODIFICATION CLAUSES

5.75 The TLC's consultation paper did not propose any regulation of duty modification clauses.[33] The consultation paper suggested that the effect of leaving duty modification clauses unregulated would be that indirect relief from liability could only be achieved by express provisions detailing the areas in which the trustees had no responsibility. If that is correct then at least it would be obvious to settlors from the face of the trust instrument what the trustee was and was not going to do. Sweeping liability exclusion clauses would be replaced by more transparent provisions establishing the trustee's area of operation.

5.76 However, we consider that this is an unduly optimistic view of the likely effect of a failure to regulate duty modification clauses as part of a statutory scheme restricting reliance on liability exclusion clauses. A trustee who wished to avoid the regulation of exclusion of liability could simply insist on the inclusion of a clause in the trust instrument modifying the standard of care owed to the beneficiaries. There would be no obvious increase in transparency. The CP's primary reform proposal would be defeated by what the CP called a "simple

---

[33] See Trust Law Committee, *Consultation Paper: Trustee Exemption Clauses* (June 1999) para 7.16.

drafting expedient".[34] One catch-all clause tucked away in the schedules to the trust instrument could simply be replaced by another one, no doubt to the ignorance of the majority of settlors.

DISTINGUISHING BETWEEN DIFFERENT SORTS OF DUTY MODIFICATION CLAUSE

5.77 The principal basis of the unpopularity of the CP's provisional proposal is that it would introduce retrospective judicial assessment of what is and is not reasonable. It was suggested to us that these difficulties could be avoided by setting out a bright line distinguishing types of duty modification clause which would and would not be subject to regulation. Such an approach would solve the avoidance problems discussed above, while leaving the majority of duty modification clauses beyond challenge, able to be relied on by trustees with certainty.

5.78 Given the aims of regulation and the preferred framing of the primary reform proposal, the obvious basis on which to distinguish between different types of clause is by reference to their effect, regulating only those clauses which have the effect of excluding liability for negligence.[35]

5.79 Some sorts of duty modification clause would be easy to categorise as having the effect of excluding liability for negligence. Most obviously, general standard of care modification clauses[36] would clearly have such an effect.

5.80 Other types of clause clearly do not have the effect of excluding liability for negligence. The CP's analysis considered extended powers clauses as a separate category of provision from duty modification clauses. On reflection, we are not convinced that this is particularly helpful as extended powers clauses can technically be seen as a type of duty modification provision.[37]

5.81 Duty modification provisions extending trustees' powers cannot on their own have the effect of removing liability for negligence. Whereas a duty requires trustees to do (or not to do) something, a power merely authorises trustees to do (or not to do) it. Trustees retain a choice as to whether or not to exercise the extended

---

[34] CP, para 4.92.

[35] A similar approach has been taken in Jersey and Guernsey, albeit with reference to gross negligence. The Trusts (Jersey) Law 1984, art 30(10) (as amended), provides that "nothing in the terms of a trust shall relieve, release or exonerate a trustee from liability for breach of trust arising from the trustee's own fraud, wilful misconduct or gross negligence". The Trusts (Guernsey) Law 1989, art 34(7) (as amended), provides that "nothing in the terms of a trust shall relieve a trustee of liability for a breach of trust arising from his own fraud or wilful misconduct or gross negligence".

[36] See para 5.53.

[37] Trustees are, as legal owners of trust property, *prima facie* entitled to exercise all the rights of the legal owner in respect of it. Trustees' freedom to deal and act is, however, subject to the general equitable duty to act in the best interests of beneficiaries and specific duties to deal or act in a particular way. A clause in a trust instrument which expressly confers a power on the trustee to do something which the trustee could not otherwise do without committing a breach of trust must therefore vary or override a default duty not to do that thing. (A clause which purports to give the trustee the power to do something which in fact the trustee could lawfully do anyway – sometimes used for the avoidance of doubt – is clearly not a duty modification clause. But such a clause is not properly described as an extended powers clause.)

power and, if they do exercise it, how to exercise it. Trustees are under a duty to exercise all their powers properly in the best interests of the beneficiaries. If they fail to do so and act negligently they will be in breach of trust. Trustees therefore remain accountable for the exercise of every power. The only way such liability could be excluded would be by additional liability exemption provisions directly protecting the trustees from the consequences of negligence (or by a general standard of care modification clause having the same effect).

5.82 Establishing the effect of some types of duty modification clause is, therefore, relatively straightforward. However, the analysis quickly becomes more difficult. We set out a full discussion of the interpretation of different sorts of duty modification clauses in Appendix D. We conclude that the correct analysis of clauses providing that "the trustee is not under a duty to do X" is that they are merely facilitative and technically do not protect trustees from liability for negligence. The effect of such clauses is, in our view, to take away the trustee's strict liability to do or not do a specified thing but not (unless they explicitly or implicitly limit the trustee's associated powers) to remove the trustee's overarching duty to exercise its powers properly. However, this analysis is not beyond dispute.

5.83 It is particularly difficult to be confident of the proper construction of certain types of duty modification clause. Some language is very difficult to analyse, for example, a clause phrased along the lines of "it is not the trustee's responsibility to do X". As Appendix D illustrates, such clauses are open to varying interpretations and much is likely to depend on the particular circumstances of the case. However, there is clearly a danger that many duty modification clauses could be held by a court to contain a protective element which must technically be classified as liability exclusion.

5.84 Like the TLC, we have been unable to find an adequate "bright line" rule to distinguish between acceptable and unacceptable duty modification provisions. The application of any statutory distinction based on the effect of the duty modification provisions would be highly complex and in many cases uncertain. The rule would invite challenge by beneficiaries and so litigation and cost. The proper interpretation might in many cases only emerge following an application to court. Consequently the likely effect of the bright line rule would be to introduce new uncertainty and all the drawbacks of the CP's provisional proposal.

5.85 These technical difficulties are not the only weakness of an approach based on a distinction between different sorts of duty modification clause. A close analysis of consultation responses suggests that, whatever the apparent support for regulation, many consultees would oppose a rule which prohibited reliance on duty modification clauses protecting the trustee from liability for negligence.

5.86 Consultation suggests that many trustees (especially those who are professionally advised) already recognise the limited protective effect of duty modification clauses and understand that they need to do more than modify their duties to escape liability. Many trustees appear to rely on expanded provisions which not only modify trustees' duties but also grant specific liability exclusion.

For example, Chapter 4 of the Financial Markets Law Committee Report[38] lists a number of standard financial market provisions which involve a degree of liability exclusion. For example, the standard clause headed "Certificate of directors or Authorised Signatories" provides that:

> The Trustee may call for and shall be at liberty to accept a certificate signed by two directors and/or two Authorised Signatories of the Issuer…as to any fact or matter *prima facie* within the knowledge of the Issuer…as sufficient evidence thereof…and the Trustee shall not be bound in any such case to call for further evidence or be responsible for any Liability that may be occasioned by its failing to do so.[39]

5.87 The first part of this clause is a form of duty modification clause (the trustee's duty to monitor is modified by an authorisation that it may rely on a certificate). However, the second part relieves the trustee of liability for relying on the authorisation even where the trustee should not have done so. The combined effect of the merged duty modification and targeted liability exclusion is therefore protective. There is no reason to think that this type of drafting (duty modification plus specific liability exclusion) is limited to commercial trusts.[40]

5.88 Consultation responses suggest that there may also be a belief (in our view mistaken) that duty modification provisions alone grant trustees blanket protection from the consequences of their actions and omissions in the relevant area of operation. Comments made in consultation appeared not to recognise the potential limitations of duty modification provisions as regards liability for the exercise (or non-exercise) of associated powers.

5.89 Consultation therefore indicated that liability exclusion often already accompanies or is thought to accompany duty modification. Legislative reform that took away the protection backing duty modification clauses would consequently have wide-reaching impact.

5.90 Indeed, this analysis may suggest that consultees' concerns about the CP's proposed treatment of duty modification clauses were not simply consequences of the terms of the proposed test of reasonableness. Any scheme based on the regulation of clauses ousting liability would give rise to similar problems, as it would open trustees' reliance on the provisions of the trust deed to subsequent scrutiny. So long as the test of negligence remained to judge the trustees' actions after the event, trustees would be unable to rely on express protections to escape the consequences.

5.91 It follows that some consultees' apparent support for the primary reform proposal's suggested regulation of liability exclusion clauses may be misleading to the extent that they opposed the CP's suggested treatment of duty modification

---

[38] Financial Markets Law Committee, *Trustee Exemption Clauses Report – Issue 62* (May 2004).

[39] See Financial Markets Law Committee, *Trustee Exemption Clauses Report – Issue 62* (May 2004) p 23.

[40] Although many trust instruments currently achieve the same effect by modifying individual duties and granting overarching (rather than targeted) liability exclusion.

clauses. Many consultees would, we believe, not be satisfied by regulation which targeted any liability exclusion element in duty modification clauses and allowed reliance only on duty modification provisions which are not protective. They would resist any regulation of trust provisions allowing trustees to take or to omit to take specified actions in the certain knowledge that they will not be held liable for doing so.

Summary

5.92 Consultation has made it apparent that the proper treatment of duty modification provisions is a vital element of any legislative reform. Although discussions of duty modification are highly technical, they are not just a theoretical nicety. If clauses which achieve indirectly what liability exclusion clauses achieve directly were not adequately regulated, it would be possible for trustees wishing to avoid regulation to do so with impunity.

5.93 The CP's provisional proposal to open up duty modification and extended powers clauses to judicial scrutiny had the advantage that it would allow the court to arrive at fact-sensitive decisions. The down-side is that it would lead to uncertainty as to whether trustees could safely rely on duty modification clauses to take or not to take specified actions. We are persuaded by consultees' arguments that that level of uncertainty would be unacceptable.

5.94 We have attempted to find a "bright line" to distinguish between duty modification clauses which would allow trustees certainty as to reliance on the clause. We have not been able to do so in a way that would avoid uncertainty and litigation.

5.95 It has emerged from our study of duty modification that many in the trust industry appear either to believe that all duty modification clauses in themselves protect trustees from liability for negligence, or to use duty modification provisions with associated liability exclusion provisions. This suggests that many trustees wish to rely on duty modification provisions to protect them from liability arising out of their own negligence. While legislation which allowed trustees to rely on duty modification provisions only to the extent that they did not authorise negligence would accord with the CP's regulatory aims, it therefore would not meet the concerns of uncertainty and inflexibility raised in consultation. We suspect that many consultees – including consultees who appeared to support the primary reform proposal – would insist that such liability exclusion was necessary in the context of duty modification clauses. This throws doubt on the real support for the meaningful regulation of trustee exemption clauses.

5.96 The CP acknowledged that the regulation of the various types of clause that can have the effect of trustee exemption is "an area of formidable difficulty where the tension between settlor freedom and beneficiary protection is very great".[41] We have not been able to overcome this difficulty.

---

[41] CP, para 4.95.

OVERALL ASSESSMENT OF THE PRINCIPAL PROVISIONAL REFORM PROPOSALS

5.97   The CP's provisional reform proposals were made with the benefit of Dr Dunn's research findings and with knowledge of the warnings of adverse regulatory impact expressed in that survey. The question, the CP suggested, "is whether in the light of these circumstances there is a strong case for intervening with the freedom of the settlor and the trustee to stipulate the terms of the trust".[42] In making its primary reform proposal the CP answered this question with a "yes".

5.98   We are no longer convinced that this is the right answer. The consultation process has provided significant support for the claims reported by Dr Dunn. It has also raised new concerns. Crucially, it has questioned the view that trustee indemnity insurance might offer an adequate alternative means of protection to trustees, and it has suggested that the CP's primary reform proposal might itself seriously affect the availability of affordable insurance. If it is correct that legislative regulation would leave many trustees without the protection of either exemption provisions or indemnity insurance, the likelihood of other adverse consequences is increased.

5.99   Although it is possible that the effects of the type of statutory intervention envisaged by the CP would not be as problematic as some consultees suggested, we have concluded that there is an unacceptably high risk that such reform would give rise to significantly damaging consequences. In particular, we consider that it could lead to increased costs for those wishing to use trusts, delays in trust administration, a greater tendency towards defensive trusteeship and a general loss of flexibility in the operation of trusts. These consequences would be to the detriment of settlors, beneficiaries, trustees and the trust industry as a whole.

5.100   The likelihood of adverse regulatory impact would be increased by the CP's suggested treatment of duty modification clauses. For the reasons discussed in detail above, we have been unable to find an adequate means of dealing with the potential avoidance of the primary reform proposal in a way which would not be likely to cause further negative consequences.

5.101   We do not believe that the danger of adverse consequences can be overcome by the adoption of any of the alternative forms of legislative regulation considered in the CP. A clear majority of consultees considered the scheme put forward in the CP preferable to alternative regulatory mechanisms. We have not been able to create a statutory scheme meeting the CP's aim of barring reliance on defined exemption clauses which does not have the potential to give rise to similar practical difficulties. Any revised legislative proposals which had the effect of raising the standard required of paid trustees would prompt similar concerns to those outlined in consultation.

5.102   In consequence we cannot recommend reform of the sort provisionally favoured by the CP. Instead, we believe that a more effective and proportionate model of regulation is to be found by concentrating upon the issue of settlor awareness

---

[42] CP, para 3.97.

and by promoting the widespread adoption of a rule of practice to effect the necessary reform. We consider the merits of such an approach in the next Part.

PART 6
REGULATION OF TRUSTEE EXEMPTION CLAUSES: A RULE OF PRACTICE

INTRODUCTION

6.1 We have considered in Part 5 the case for and against the CP's principal provisional proposals for the legislative regulation of trustee exemption clauses.

6.2 In this Part we consider the case for alternative forms of regulation. Rather than seeking to intervene in the relationship between the trustee and the beneficiary, these alternative approaches focus on the relationship between the trustee and the settlor. Specifically, we consider regulation aimed at ensuring that settlors are aware of the meaning and effect of exemption provisions when settling assets on trust. We conclude that this issue of what we refer to as "settlor awareness" can best be addressed by means of promotion of a rule of practice applicable to paid trustees, adopted by regulatory bodies, and enforceable by disciplinary sanctions.

THE PROBLEM OF SETTLOR AWARENESS

6.3 A common criticism of the current law is that some settlors execute a trust instrument containing a trustee exemption clause without being fully aware of its effect, and possibly even its existence. Many of those who responded to the CP pointed to an asymmetry of information between settlors and trustees whereby many settlors fail to understand a key component of the bargain negotiated with paid trustees for their professional services. If, as we believe, a powerful justification for upholding trustee exemption clauses is to respect the autonomy of the settlor, steps should be taken to ensure that the inclusion of such clauses is indeed a manifestation of that autonomy, and not something that has happened by accident rather than design.

6.4 The fact that a settlor does not appreciate the precise effect of certain trust provisions is not enough to invalidate the trust. A settlor must have sufficient intention to create a trust. However, this does not require a detailed understanding of all the trust's terms. Probate will only be granted in accordance with the terms of a will trust if the court is satisfied that the testator "knew and approved" of its contents at the time of execution. The doctrine of knowledge and approval is, however, relatively rigid and inflexible and has been applied most frequently where those claiming benefits under the will have been responsible for its preparation.[1] It does not require proof that the testator knew of the legal effects of the will. We are not aware of any cases where a trustee exemption clause in a will trust has been challenged on the grounds of lack of knowledge and approval.

6.5 As things stand, prospective trustees are not specifically required to make the settlor aware of exemption provisions in the trust deed. This remains the case

---

[1] See, for instance, *Wintle v Nye* [1959] 1 WLR 284, and, generally, *Theobald on Wills* (16th ed 2001) para 3-11 and following.

even where the trustee has been responsible for drafting the trust or where the instrument is in the trustee's standard form.[2]

6.6 The position is apparently not altered by the fact that the prospective trustee also acts as an adviser to the settlor (or is otherwise in a fiduciary relationship with him). In *Bogg v Raper*,[3] a solicitor trustee successfully invoked the protection of a trustee exemption clause in a will trust where he had both drafted the trust and advised the testator. It was argued that the trustee was in breach of his fiduciary duty in obtaining the benefit of exemption and so should be prevented from relying on the exemption clause (unless he could prove that the testator had received full and independent advice about its effects). Millett LJ considered there to be a "fundamental fallacy" in this argument, as the exemption clause did not confer a benefit on the person advising the testator on the contents of his will. Therefore, the inclusion of the clause in the will was not a transaction in which the testator and his advisor had conflicting interests.[4]

6.7 There is consequently a concern that many settlors do not realise that their trusts contain provisions conferring wide protections on their trustees. Although sensible settlors will read the trust deed as a matter of course and take advice on any aspects they do not understand, exemption provisions are particularly susceptible to oversight. Trustee exemption clauses often appear in a schedule towards the end of the trust instrument, surrounded by a greater or lesser amount of legal boilerplate. The effect of such clauses is obvious to anyone who has been alerted to the issue, but their full implications can easily be lost on a reader dealing with the complexities of trusts for the first time.

6.8 The impression that settlors may not fully appreciate the import of trustee exemption clauses is supported by Dr Dunn's socio-economic research. This found that settlors are generally not well informed about or particularly concerned with trustee exemption clauses, considering such clauses to be largely "administrative" provisions.[5]

6.9 A number of consultees pressed for regulation addressing the specific issue of settlor awareness. They argued that reform of this sort would prevent the inclusion of exemption clauses in the trust instrument without the informed consent of the settlor while allowing reliance on such provisions where the settlor considers it appropriate.

---

[2] In *Bogg v Raper* (1998/99) 1 ITELR 267, Millett LJ refers in passing to the consequences of a solicitor-trustee drafting a trust, deliberately concealing the existence of an exemption clause from the settlor and then seeking to rely upon the clause. It is unclear to what, and how far, Millett LJ's comments (which did not form part of his decision on the facts in this case) were intended to apply. However, it is likely that they were intended to reflect the wider principle in *Armitage v Nurse* that a trustee cannot rely on an exemption clause where there is fraud. They arguably apply this principle to the fraudulent insertion of exemption clauses. However, this element of the judgment in *Bogg v Raper* certainly does not provide a clear basis for believing that all trustees who draft trusts have a legal duty to disclose the meaning and effect of exemption clauses to their settlors.

[3] (1998/99) 1 ITELR 267.

[4] See paras 2.18 to 2.20.

[5] See CP, para 3.37 and following, and para 4.42.

6.10 We agree. Targeted regulation focusing on the disclosure of exemption clauses would increase the transparency of those provisions, while reinforcing the important principle of settlor autonomy. It would address the most pressing weakness of the current law and the cases of greatest unfairness, while avoiding the difficulties that have persuaded us against wider regulation of the sort provisionally proposed in the CP.

A REJECTION OF STATUTORY DISCLOSURE REQUIREMENTS

6.11 It would be possible to introduce such regulation by legislative means. Statute could prohibit reliance on a trustee exemption clause unless the trustees could show that they had taken specified steps to bring the clause to the attention of the settlor. Indeed, the approach suggested by the TLC in their consultation paper placed important emphasis on settlor awareness. They proposed that their preferred form of statutory regulation of trustee exemption clauses should not apply:

> ... where it is proved that before the creation of the trust the settlor was given advice in writing, by a person reasonably competent in drafting trust documentation, and independent of the proposed trustee of the trust, drawing the settlor's attention to the scope and effect of the provision concerned.[6]

6.12 The TLC justified this approach on the basis of settlor autonomy and the need for trusts to remain sufficiently flexible to meet the demands of the different purposes to which they are put.

The CP's settlor-oriented statutory options

6.13 The CP gave consultees the opportunity to comment on the option of a statutory prohibition on reliance on exemption clauses which had not been validated by a formality or procedural requirement.[7] A number of alternatives were considered.[8] However, the CP rejected the view that formality requirements should play a primary role in the legislative regulation of trustee exemption clauses. The vast majority of consultees agreed with the rejection of this approach.

6.14 The CP and consultation outlined three main problems with a legislative scheme whereby the effect of complying with a formality requirement would be to validate a clause which was presumptively invalid.

Additional time and cost

6.15 A number of consultees warned that such a statutory scheme would make trusts significantly slower, more inconvenient and therefore more expensive to set up.

---

[6] See Trust Law Committee, *Consultation Paper: Trustee Exemption Clauses* (June 1999) para 7.18.

[7] CP, para 4.41 and following.

[8] Eg requiring settlors to sign a form to verify that the trust instrument was executed after the exemption clause had been brought to their notice and explained, requiring settlors to be offered an alternative trust without an exemption clause, requiring that settlors receive legal advice (or independent legal advice) on the effect of the exemption clause.

6.16 Consultees concentrated their comments on what was widely seen as the most likely form of statutory formality requirement: a requirement that the settlor take independent legal advice prior to execution of the trust instrument. This was generally considered to be unduly onerous.

6.17 They pointed out that independent advisers would have to take on prospective settlors as new clients. This would involve all the usual procedures, including ever-tightening money laundering requirements. The extent of disclosure required would depend on the scope of the statutory regulation (which is discussed in more detail in paragraph 6.28 and following). However, it is likely that advisers would have to acquaint themselves at least to some degree with all the provisions of the proposed trust deed before they could properly explain the effect of the relevant clause or clauses.

6.18 The provision of the required advice would therefore be a significant undertaking. Where the independent adviser had experience of a particular standard form trust, economies of scale would no doubt apply. In many cases, however, the cost of independent advice could be wholly out of proportion to the other costs of setting up the trust. By adding a new layer of expense, the formality could prejudice the competitiveness of the trust model as against alternative arrangements.

6.19 The effect of delay should also not be underestimated. Although many trusts do not have to be set up in a great hurry, delays might nevertheless put some settlors off making trusts. On occasion (especially where the trust is to be contained in a will), delay could be critical.

6.20 Of course, legislative regulation of formality requirements would not necessarily have to specify independent advice. If the key statutory principle were that the settlor should be aware of the trustee exemption clause and its effects, it would be sufficient that the settlor had been appropriately advised even where there was no written confirmation; the fact of the advice would be determinative, rather than compliance with any prescribed formality.

6.21 However, so long as the consequence of failure to comply with statutory requirements would be to prevent reliance on an exemption provision, we very much doubt that the problems of cost and delay would be overcome. From the trustee's point of view, the potential consequences would make the risk of such a loss of protection a very serious matter. The fear of a finding of non-compliance would, we believe, drive trustees to insist on practices that provided cast-iron proof of compliance. In many cases, this would include independent advice. The overall effect would remain disproportionate to the aims of regulation.

Evidential difficulties

6.22 We have outlined why we believe that a statutory scheme requiring specified steps to validate an exemption clause would cause trustees to put in place rigorous procedures to protect their interests. Consultees suggested that in some circumstances even these procedures might not be enough to avoid disputes about statutory compliance.

6.23 A number warned that it was in practice inevitable that documentary evidence would occasionally be lost, or in some way rendered questionable. The potential for evidential difficulties would be pronounced where a trust had continued over a long period, with a number of changes of trustee. Consultees observed that a trust may have been set up decades before any issue as to the validity of an exemption clause arose. If there were not complete and accurate records, then the distant memories of relevant persons would become crucial, assuming that they were still alive. Any dispute about the original trustee's compliance would be time-consuming and costly.

6.24   It is difficult to know how much weight to place on these concerns. Clearly, there is an argument that paid professional trustees ought to be able to avoid such problems by applying appropriate procedures. However, we accept that there is some potential for difficulties, especially given the timescales involved. Of course, evidential difficulties of this sort would not just cause problems to trustees seeking to rely on exemption provisions. They would also impact on any beneficiary wishing to challenge a clause on the basis that the settlor had not been made properly aware of its inclusion in the trust instrument.

Lack of certainty

6.25   Elsewhere in this Report we outline a number of concerns about the effect of introducing a reasonableness test, either for duty modification clauses in particular or for exemption clauses generally.[9] Consultees suggested that such a test would give rise to unacceptable uncertainty as it would open trustees' reliance on trust terms to subsequent legal challenge. A statutory scheme requiring specified steps to validate exemption clauses could have similar effects.

6.26   One could argue that it is a problem of the trustee's own making if it fails to take sufficient steps to provide proof of settlor awareness of the clause. However, the trustee seeking reliance on the clause would often not be the trustee who oversaw the instigation of the trust. The rights and duties of the trustee may live on for many years after the original trustees have ceased to act. A successor trustee would not be aware of the precise circumstances surrounding the creation of the trust and would have to investigate a procedure that may have taken place many years earlier. New trustees might be deterred from acting by uncertainty over the validity of an exemption clause, even if in fact the clause would be held to be valid.

6.27   This uncertainty would also operate against the interests of beneficiaries. In many cases, they, like the trustee, could not be certain as to what may have been said or done many years earlier and so could not be certain as to the status of particular clauses. As a result, neither party could be confident as to the effective terms of the trust, and neither could wholly rely on the apparent terms of the trust instrument.

Duty modification clauses

6.28   We have discussed in detail the complexities of duty modification clauses.[10] In particular, we have addressed the difficulties of regulating those types of duty

---

[9]   See para 5.38 and following, and Appendix A, para A.9 and following.

[10]   See para 5.46 and following.

modification clause which could be used to avoid statutory controls on liability exclusion, without impacting on duty modification clauses which have an entirely proper purpose and which genuinely define the scope of the trustee's role.

6.29 Similar issues would arise in formulating a statutory scheme aimed at ensuring settlor awareness by denying reliance on trustee exemption clauses that had not been adequately disclosed. Any statutory requirement to make the settlor aware of exemption clauses in the trust instrument would have to specify the kind of clauses which would be subject to this requirement. It would have to address duty modification clauses in order to prevent avoidance. The problems presented by the complexities of the operation of duty modification clauses would be different from those discussed in relation to the type of scheme provisionally proposed by the CP; any clauses could be relied upon if disclosed to the settlor. However, the difficulty of identifying which clauses required disclosure and explaining their operation to settlors should not be underestimated.

6.30 The statutory scheme could require disclosure of all provisions having the effect of removing liability for negligence.[11] However, the difficulties of identifying whether a particular duty modification clause has that technical effect, discussed in detail in Part 5 and Appendix D, would remain. Trustees would have to carry out the complicated analysis of all duty modifying provisions before they could be sure which clauses needed to be disclosed.

6.31 It could be argued that the difficulties of this analysis could be overcome by a legislative requirement that all duty modification clauses should be disclosed to the settlor, whatever their technical effect. However, this would still require the trustee to identify which provisions were duty modification clauses. Any clause in a trust deed which renders the duties of the trustee different from those that would otherwise apply can be considered a duty modification clause. Every clause in the trust instrument would therefore have to be individually analysed and some clauses would be likely to be ambiguous in their effect.[12] In some cases, such a requirement might lead the trustee to disclose the majority of the terms of the trust.

6.32 We therefore believe that the technical problems presented by duty modification clauses would have a significant impact on any statutory scheme seeking to regulate reliance on exemption clauses. When the trustee's ability to rely on the exemption clause is at stake, the trustee would be forced to undertake the complex analysis of such clauses and make potentially wide-ranging disclosure to the settlor.

Conclusion

6.33 We agree with the conclusion of the majority of consultees that the statutory formality requirements discussed in the CP would be likely to give rise to additional time and cost on setting up a trust and to uncertainty thereafter.

---

[11] In line with the discussion at para 5.77 and following.

[12] For example, a clause stating "the trustee shall have the power to do X" could be a duty modification clause if the trustee would not otherwise be entitled to do X. If, however, the trustee already had the power to do X as a matter of general law then the clause would merely confirm this, and not be a duty modification clause.

Evidential difficulties might also arise, albeit rarely. Furthermore, it is not clear how such a statutory requirement could adequately frame the regulation of duty modification clauses.

A more developed settlor-oriented statutory scheme

6.34 The CP suggested drawing a strict line between cases where the settlor had and had not been made aware of the exemption clause. In the former, the trustee could rely on the exemption clause; in the latter, the trustee could not.

6.35 This scheme could be refined in a variety of ways. For example, it would be possible to blend the requirement of settlor awareness with a test of reasonableness. Such a scheme could work by preventing the trustees from relying on an exemption clause which is not, as against the settlor, a reasonable one to be included in the trust deed. The settlor-focus of the scheme would be achieved by basing the test of reasonableness primarily on transparency.[13] An exemption clause would generally be considered reasonable if it was explained to the settlor, and the settlor agreed to its inclusion. In addition, a clause would automatically be deemed to be reasonable if the settlor was acting in the course of business or was being independently legally advised on the terms of the trust.[14] Substantive principles of reasonableness would then apply to clauses which were not explained to the settlor, and a trustee would be unable to rely on an unreasonable clause.[15]

6.36 To an even greater extent than other statutory settlor-oriented schemes, this type of approach would avoid many of the problems undermining the CP's primary reform proposal.[16] For example, trustees would be much less likely to act defensively if presented with a means of obtaining a degree of certainty as to whether they could rely on exemption provisions. There would be less reluctance to accept trusteeship if transparent exemption clauses could be relied upon. There would not be a significant increase in trust litigation, since the enforceability of most exemption clauses would be apparent.

6.37 Furthermore, this approach could potentially ease some of the difficulties associated with the CP's settlor-oriented option.

(1) *Additional time and cost*: Trustees might derive some comfort from being able to rely on a reasonable exemption clause whether or not they had

[13] This is similar to the "fair and reasonable" test set out in the Law Commission and Scottish Law Commission's draft Unfair Contract Terms Bill, cl 14. This states that whether a contract term is fair and reasonable is to be determined by taking into account the extent to which it is transparent, its substance and effect, and the circumstances at the time it was agreed. See Unfair Terms in Contracts (2005) Law Com No 292; Scot Law Com No 199, Appendix A.

[14] Ensuring that the settlor had independent legal advice would therefore provide a "safe harbour" for a trustee concerned about the reasonableness and consequent enforceability of an exemption clause.

[15] The trustees would therefore be able to rely on an exemption clause unless the settlor was not acting in the course of business and did not have independent legal advice, the clause was not explained to the settlor, and the clause was substantively unreasonable as against the settlor.

[16] As discussed in paras 5.12 to 5.37.

explained it to the settlor. However, it is likely that many trustees would wish to ensure that they had cast-iron proof of compliance and so independent legal advice might commonly be insisted upon in order to take advantage of the "safe harbour" provision.

(2) *Evidential difficulties*: The potential for evidential difficulties would be diminished by applying a test of transparency-based reasonableness rather than a strict test of disclosure to the settlor. It would therefore be open to trustees (and successor trustees) to rely on any evidence which indicated that the clause was a reasonable clause to include in the trust deed. This would include any available proof of explanation to the settlor, but would not be limited to such evidence.

(3) *Lack of certainty*: Any approach which allows the possibility of exemption clauses being invalidated has the potential to undermine certainty. However, a more sophisticated scheme along the lines of that discussed above would offer trustees various means of ensuring certain reliance on such clauses. By ensuring that the settlor received independent legal advice or dealing in circumstances where the settlor was acting in the course of business the trustees would be able to rely on exemption clauses without challenge.

6.38 We therefore believe that a sophisticated statutory approach could ameliorate some of the problems associated with settlor-oriented formalities-based statutory regulation. However, we believe that to some extent these problems are inherent in any statutory scheme, however sophisticated, which renders trustees' ability to rely on an exemption clause uncertain.

6.39 The complexities associated with duty modification clauses, in particular, would remain an obstacle to any statutory approach which could bar reliance on them. Any such statutory scheme would have to overcome the difficulties of identifying duty modification clauses, analysing their effects, and distinguishing those performing a legitimate duty-defining function from those seeking to circumvent restrictions on liability exclusion.[17]

6.40 While we do not dismiss the possibility that a sophisticated statutory approach to ensuring settlor awareness could operate effectively, we remain unconvinced that such a scheme could satisfactorily overcome all the defects described above, and, in particular, maintain certainty for the trustees while minimising costs.

A NON-STATUTORY APPROACH

6.41 While rejecting a statutory formalities approach, the CP considered that "those advising a settlor (whether or not they are also trustees) should be expected, as a matter of good practice, to bring the attention of their client to any trustee exemption clause and to explain its legal consequences".[18] It appears from the written responses of consultees and from other comments received that there is widespread agreement with this sentiment.

---

[17] See para 5.46 and following, para 6.28 and following, and Appendix D.

[18] CP, para 4.45.

6.42 A number of consultees expressly indicated their preference for a strengthened formulation, going beyond simple guidance as to good practice. For example, Lord Walker of Gestingthorpe said "I would strengthen 'good practice' to 'professional duty'". Michael Jacobs[19] agreed:

> The ethical guidelines issued to solicitors are not clear on this subject, and there is a remarkable lack of professional guidance to solicitor trustees on the conflicts of interest which may regularly arise where a solicitor is either an adviser to the person establishing the trust of which he is to become a trustee or an adviser to the trustees as a body when he is also a trustee. This is something I feel strongly the Law Society should review. However it is not a matter for statutory regulation. It would be desirable for the professional bodies regulating the activities of other professional advisers to undertake a parallel review with the Law Society in respect of their own professions.

6.43 While sharing the same policy aims as a statutory disclosure requirement, a rule of practice would operate in a significantly different way. Compliance with the rule would be a matter of professional conduct for the trustee. The consequence of non-compliance in respect of a particular clause would not be to invalidate or in any way affect reliance on that clause. Rather it would be to render the trustee open to professional disciplinary measures.

6.44 The decision whether to invoke disciplinary sanctions would be in the hands of the relevant regulatory body.[20] Such bodies would be in a wholly different position from a court asked to rule on whether or not a trustee could rely on a particular protection to escape liability. The regulator's concern would be to promote compliance with the spirit of the rule and the wider aims of regulation. The regulator would consequently be unlikely to be overly concerned with unintentional, minor or technical breaches, provided the trustee had acted with reasonable care and in good faith.[21]

6.45 So long as the rule was applied flexibly and the effect of a breach was not to strip away the protection on which the trustee had been relying, we believe that the problems associated with a statutory disclosure scheme could be largely overcome.

6.46 Trustees would be less likely to introduce time-consuming and expensive processes aimed at ensuring incontrovertible proof of compliance. They would be able to take steps appropriate to the circumstances of individual settlors, rather

---

[19] Founder member and Executive Committee member, formerly Secretary, of the Trust Law Committee.

[20] See para 6.51 and following for a detailed discussion of the potential operation of such a rule.

[21] The most severe remedies would be likely to be applied only where there was sharp practice or repeated breach.

than concern themselves with the possibility of a wide-ranging forensic investigation.[22] This would minimise the danger of unnecessary cost and delay.

6.47   A rule of practice would avoid the evidential difficulties and uncertainty outlined above. The rule would not have the potential to haunt the trust long after the relevant parties (that is the settlor and the original trustee) had dropped out of the picture. Where the original trustee had not acted properly that trustee would be liable to professional sanction whether or not it continued as trustee and whether or not there was a breach of trust. The rule would have no application to successor trustees.

6.48   We therefore believe that a rule of practice requiring trustees to disclose trustee exemption provisions would work better than a statutory scheme barring reliance on exemption provisions except where trustees had made such disclosure. That there would be no bar to reliance is particularly important in enabling the difficulties presented by duty modification clauses to be overcome. While we accept that a practice-based approach has its own inherent limitations, we believe that its operation would be proportionate to the aims and objectives of regulation.

6.49   We have given careful consideration to the possible application of a rule of practice. We have consulted widely with professional bodies and trust industry organisations, with a view to developing this approach and securing its implementation.[23] We have also spoken to the TLC, whose own consultation paper influenced the referral of trustee exemption clauses to the Law Commission.[24] The TLC have indicated to us that they broadly support our rule of practice.

6.50   We have concluded in the light of our discussions that a rule of practice would offer an appropriate means of improving current trustee practice concerning exemption clauses and of overcoming the most unsatisfactory examples of their use. We consider the formulation of our favoured rule at paragraph 6.65. However, before we do so, it is important that we outline how we consider such a rule could be best implemented.

Operation of the rule

6.51   Our discussion of statutory settlor-oriented schemes of regulation has not focused on who should be responsible for satisfying the stipulated disclosure requirements.[25] A rule of practice operates differently and must specify which parties are subject to the rule.

---

[22]   In order to help prevent disproportionately expensive efforts to comply with the rule in difficult circumstances, we propose that the requirement should be to take such steps as are reasonable. See paras 6.73 and following.

[23]   A complete list of the organisations and individuals we have consulted can be found in Appendix F.

[24]   See para 1.6.

[25]   Such schemes simply dictate the consequences of non-compliance (the exemption provision being rendered ineffective) which fall on the trustee.

6.52   We consider that the rule of practice should apply as widely as possible in order to maximise its effect in raising settlor awareness. For that reason, we believe that the rule should apply both to those who draft trusts[26] and to paid trustees.

6.53   Most of those who draft trusts are regulated professionals. However, unlike some other jurisdictions,[27] there is currently no overarching system of non-legislative regulation of trustees in England and Wales.[28] Specifically, there is no requirement for trustees to register or to be licensed to practise as trustee. It would not be appropriate to create such a system solely in order to regulate the disclosure of trustee exemption clauses and ensure compliance with such regulation. There is therefore no vehicle for a single catch-all rule of practice to which all trustees would automatically be subject.

6.54   Nevertheless, there are means whereby the rule of practice could be made to govern the majority of trustees. Many of those who act as trustee are subject to regulation because of their status or activities. For example, solicitor trustees are subject to the Solicitors' Practice Rules.[29] To the extent that our proposed rule were adopted by such regulators, all regulated persons would automatically be subject to the rule when acting as trustee.

6.55   Regulatory bodies have various methods of policing compliance with their rules. It would also be open to interested parties (including the settlor and beneficiaries) to bring breaches to the attention of the governing body. The consequences of a regulated person's failure to comply would depend on the penalties available to the relevant governing body. While few governing bodies would have the power to order compensation to the beneficiaries,[30] a number of sanctions would be available. Non-compliant trustees might be liable to public censure, fines and ultimately expulsion from membership and the removal of authorisation to act.

6.56   There is therefore a vehicle for ensuring that regulated trustees are governed by our rule. In addition, many trustees are members of industry associations and similar organisations.[31] Membership is entered into voluntarily (in order to take advantage of marketing, networking and educational opportunities). However,

---

[26]   Where the drafter of a trust is in a professional-client relationship with the settlor it may as a matter of general law be negligent for the drafter not to bring the clause to the attention of the settlor. The application of the rule to those drafting trusts develops the recommendation of good practice made in the CP that those advising a settlor should bring the attention of their client to any trustee exemption clause.

[27]   The Guernsey Financial Services Commission has issued a Code of Practice for Trust Service Providers. This is not legally binding, but may be taken into account by the Commission when exercising its powers. The Jersey Financial Services Commission has issued its Trust Company Business: Codes of Practice. This has a similar status and effect to the Guernsey Code of Practice. In each case, the Financial Services Commission can refuse registration to a trust service provider which does not comply with its code.

[28]   But see para 6.124 and following on possible future developments.

[29]   See http://www.lawsociety.org.uk/professional/conduct.law (last visited 16 June 2006). There are currently 132,901 solicitors on the Roll of the Law Society of England and Wales, 6,315 of whom undertake trust work, and 13,936 wills and probate.

[30]   Whether compensation can be awarded varies between the professional bodies. If compensation cannot be compulsorily awarded, the trustee may voluntarily pay compensation in order to protect its position.

[31]   For example, STEP has over 4,500 UK trusts and estates practitioner members in the UK.

membership brings with it a greater or lesser degree of regulation. Some of these organisations have rules of conduct.[32] Others operate under the general principle that membership can be refused or withdrawn where appropriate. We believe that these types of organisation should also promote the proposed rule of practice to their members. This would give further impetus to the general acceptance of good practice.

6.57   We believe that our discussions with regulatory bodies and trust organisations will lead to the widespread adoption of our rule of practice. Given the regulatory backdrop, we believe that the rule could be adopted by the trust industry as follows.

Bespoke rules

6.58   Discussions between the Law Commission and a selection of professional and regulatory bodies suggest that a number of organisations would be willing and able to introduce regulation on the basis of the recommendations of this Report. Such bodies would create their own bespoke rule of practice, incorporating the elements described below[33] but adapted to meet the particular needs of their membership and their regulatory structure. The effect of introducing the rule into these bodies' existing rules would be that regulated individuals would automatically be subject to the rule when acting as trustee.

6.59   As a direct result of our discussions, some organisations have already moved towards formally introducing rules[34] for their own members:

(1)   the Law Society of England and Wales is considering adapting the guidance to the professional rules which may apply in this context;

(2)   the Institute of Chartered Accountants in England and Wales is drafting guidance for its members on the duty to disclose trustee exemption clauses arising from the fundamental principle of integrity required by the Institute's Code of Ethics; and

(3)   the England and Wales region of STEP has completed this process, and is the first organisation to have produced a rule in its final, authorised form.

6.60   We reproduce STEP's rule of practice in Appendix G.

---

[32]   For example, STEP has its own Code of Professional Conduct, which members are required to abide by, and an Ethics and Discipline Committee which deals with breaches of the Code.

[33]   Para 6.65 and following.

[34]   We have, as a result of our discussions with regulatory bodies, become aware of some sensitivity to the term "rule". In many regulatory systems, "rules" generally describe fundamental, high-level principles. In such systems the type of regulation we are proposing would normally be implemented as guidance on the application of a fundamental principle (eg acting in the best interests of the client or behaving with integrity in all professional and business relationships). Such guidance is indirectly binding as the regulator has power to demand justification for any departure from the guidance. This may give rise to disciplinary measures based on breach of the fundamental principle.

Statement of the rule

6.61 We recognise that not all trust and other relevant organisations have the resources or existing regulatory structure to create a bespoke rule of practice for their membership. There are also trustees who are not regulated at all but who would be willing to comply with the rule.

6.62 We therefore believe that it would be advantageous for us to set out a statement of the rule. This would outline the key elements of the rule, and provide guidance on its intended application, as a stand-alone statement of good practice.

6.63 This statement of the rule would not have automatic regulatory effect and would not carry penalties for non-compliance. It would instead be made available to regulators for wholesale adoption or incorporation into existing codes of conduct, and to unregulated trustees as guidance on best practice.

6.64 We anticipate that this statement of the rule would perform a subsidiary role. Where an organisation is able to produce, and incorporate into its existing regulatory framework, its own bespoke rule of practice, it should be encouraged to do so. Furthermore, the precise content of our statement of the rule should not be perceived as a constraint on the ability of such bodies to adapt the rule of practice to their own circumstances.

The rule

6.65 Any paid trustee who causes a settlor to include a clause in a trust instrument which has the effect of excluding or limiting liability for negligence must before the creation of the trust take such steps as are reasonable to ensure that the settlor is aware of the meaning and effect of the clause.

6.66 Some of the elements of this formulation require further explanation. Similar explanation should be provided by regulatory and professional bodies to their members as guidance on bespoke versions of the rule.

"Paid trustee"

6.67 As Part 4 made clear, we have concluded that any regulation should focus on trustees who receive payment in respect of their services as trustees. "Paid" should be interpreted flexibly so as to take account of indirect financial benefits. Regulated professionals should be required to take all reasonable steps to procure that any company or partnership in which they have a financial interest comply with the rule.

6.68 We have explained that we have designed this statement of the rule for use by trustees not governed by bespoke regulation. For this reason, it concentrates on the responsibility of trustees. However, we recommend that regulatory and professional bodies whose membership includes the drafters of trusts should extend regulation to those who draft trust documentation containing trustee exemption provisions.[35]

---

[35] STEP follows this approach in para 1 of its rule: see Appendix G

"Causes the settlor to include a clause"

6.69   We recognise that it is the settlor who establishes the terms of the trust when executing the trust instrument. The rule therefore applies when a trustee "causes" a settlor to include a clause in a trust instrument.

6.70   A prospective trustee should be considered to have caused the inclusion of the term where it has (i) drafted the trust in its capacity as the settlor's adviser; (ii) provided the settlor with a standard form trust; or (iii) requested or required an exemption clause during the course of negotiations over its proposed trusteeship.

6.71   Where more than one trustee is to be appointed and one or more of the prospective trustees requests or requires the inclusion of a trustee exemption clause, the rule should apply to all prospective trustees. We recognise that there may be situations where a particular regulated prospective trustee is not the party pushing for the exemption clause. Nevertheless, that regulated person will on appointment potentially benefit from the protection of the clause and we believe it is not unfair in such circumstances to expect that person to take responsibility for disclosure of the clause to the settlor. However, it may be reasonable for the regulated prospective trustees to take no further steps to make the settlor aware of the meaning and effect of the clause where they believe in good faith that another prospective trustee has taken reasonable steps to do so.

"Trust instrument"

6.72   The rule is intended to apply in relation to all types of trust instrument, including trusts contained in wills. References to "settlors" should be taken to include "testators" where appropriate.

"Such steps as are reasonable"

6.73   The rule requires the trustee to take "such steps as are reasonable". In some circumstances it would be reasonable for the trustee not to take any steps at all. The rule should only be seen to require the trustee to act so far as is practicable, so that trustees will not be liable for any failure to act where they were unable to do what would otherwise have been required. The requirement that the trustee take "such steps as are reasonable" has a number of elements.

FORM OF THE DISCLOSURE

6.74   The precise steps required of the trustee are not specified. There is no requirement for independent advice. The concern the rule seeks to address is that the settlor may be unaware of the existence or the import of the trustee exemption clause. We see no reason why it should not be the trustees themselves who point this out to the settlor. The concern is a lack of knowledge and understanding rather than a fear of undue influence. In the majority of cases, trustees (or their advisers) are best placed to provide the advice, having suggested or required the inclusion of the relevant clause in the trust instrument. In some circumstances, the trustee might consider independent advice appropriate. However, this should not be as a matter of course.

6.75   Our statement of the rule does not require the trustee to provide written advice. It would consequently be open to a trustee to comply with its obligations by discussing the relevant clause with the settlor in person or on the telephone.

74

However, we do not recommend such practice, and note that it could lead to difficulties in the event of any future suggestion of non-compliance.

"ENSURE THAT THE SETTLOR IS AWARE"

6.76   Although we have on occasion used the term "disclose" as a shorthand for the action required by the rule, the phrase "ensure the settlor is aware" imposes a slightly more onerous requirement. The trustee must consider the likely experience of the settlor and attempt to convey the meaning and legal effect of the relevant clause in a way so as to make the settlor understand what he or she is being told.

6.77   Of course, it will often be difficult for trustees to assess a particular settlor's capacity to understand the meaning and effect of an exemption clause or the effect of their attempts at explanation. This could leave trustees uncertain as to whether they had complied with their duty were it not for the fact that the rule only requires trustees to take "such steps as are reasonable". Provided therefore that trustees have acted reasonably they will have satisfied the rule.

CIRCUMSTANCES WHERE NO ACTION NECESSARY

6.78   There are a number of circumstances in which we consider it would not be reasonably necessary for the trustee to do anything. The range of factors justifying non-disclosure may be quite wide, and the following list is not intended to be comprehensive. Other factors which may be significant include the trustees' previous dealings with the settlor and their knowledge of the settlor's experience in trust matters.

Settlor is independently legally advised

6.79   Where the settlor is being independently legally advised on the terms of the trust, it is reasonable for a prospective trustee to assume that the adviser will draw the settlor's attention to any exemption provisions. We consequently do not consider it necessary for the trustee to take any steps to do so.

"Commercial" trusts[36]

6.80   A significant feature of consultation was the message that many of the CP's arguments in favour of trustee exemption clauses were inapplicable to commercial trusts, for example, on the basis that the settlors of such trusts tend to be market equals of the trustee and so are in less need of protection.

6.81   Not all of the arguments in favour of excluding commercial trusts from a statutory scheme apply to our revised policy recommendation of a rule of practice. Indeed, in many cases compliance with the rule would not require any change to current market practice. It is already standard practice in many commercial trust situations for information to be provided to settlors about exemption and similar provisions.[37] Compliance with the rule would also not be an issue in cases where

---

[36]   See Appendix C, para C.33 and following for a more general discussion of the need for regulation of commercial trusts.

[37]   For example, in bond issue prospectuses.

it was clear that the experience of the settlor was such that advice was unnecessary or where the settlor was in receipt of independent legal advice.

6.82 However, we recognise that it would be useful for commercial trustees to be given further general guidance on when they would be expected to take steps to make an exemption clause disclosure. While it would be possible (and, in the context of a statutory rule, essential) to draw up detailed rules dealing with the miscellany of commercial trust situations, we believe that it is sufficient to confirm that the rule is of no effect in two circumstances:

(1) *Where the trustee is subject to statutory regulation of trustee exemption provisions*: This would exclude trustees of debentures[38] and authorised unit trust schemes[39] from the scope of the rule, on the basis that the rule would be unnecessary where an exemption clause can be rendered void by statute; and

(2) *Where the settlor acts in the course of business*: More widely, it would be reasonable for the trustee not to take any steps where the settlor is acting in the course of business, unless it ought reasonably to be apparent to the trustee that the transaction is an unusual transaction for the settlor to enter into. This is likely to apply to the majority of corporate settlors and to some individuals.

Pension trusts[40]

6.83 Pensions are to a great extent a law unto themselves. They are conceptually different from other trusts and operate in a distinct manner. They are, for example, already subject to the pensions regulator, created by the Pensions Act 2004.

6.84 As we discuss in Appendix C,[41] application of the draft rule to pensions would be difficult and, we believe, ineffective. The settlor in an occupational pension scheme is the employer, who is usually legally advised and who should therefore as a matter of course be made aware of any exemption clause. There is a strong argument that the beneficiaries of such a scheme, who contribute to the fund financially or by their employment service, should also be treated as settlors. However, a requirement that scheme members should be advised as to the meaning and effect of exemption provisions in the pension trust would serve no practical purpose. Employees are rarely presented with a choice of occupational pension and are therefore not usually able to choose one without an exemption clause.

6.85 We therefore consider that the rule of practice should be of no application in the context of pension trusts.

---

[38] Companies Act 1985, s 192: see para 2.30.

[39] Financial Services and Markets Act 2000, s 253: see para 2.28.

[40] See Appendix C, para C.16 and following for a more general discussion of the need for regulation of pension trusts.

[41] See Appendix C, para C.32.

Charitable trusts[42]

6.86   In many cases our draft rule will be inapplicable to charitable trusts on the basis either that they do not include a trustee exemption clause[43] or that the trustees are not remunerated.

6.87   However, the rule will *prima facie* be of application to some charitable trusts where there is a paid trustee and an exemption clause. In such cases, the operation of the rule is not entirely straightforward. It could be argued that every donor to a charity should be viewed as a settlor for the purposes of the rule. However, giving the required explanation to all donors would be wholly impractical.

6.88   We therefore consider that the rule should only be engaged in relation to the original settlor of a charitable trust who is involved in the establishment of the terms of the trust.

6.89   The Charity Commission has indicated that it will be considering an appropriate response to the recommendations of this Report.

"Meaning and effect of the clause"

6.90   The rule requires the trustee to do more than simply disclose the existence of any trustee exemption clause. It calls for an explanation of the meaning and effect of the clause. The term "meaning and effect" is intended to require that the trustee explains what the clause means in plain English and points out its potential consequences in the event of a breach of trust.

Duty modification clauses

6.91   We have taken the policy decision that regulation is only necessary for clauses having the effect of excluding liability for negligence. For this reason, we do not recommend that the rule of practice should require disclosure of all duty modification clauses.[44]

6.92   The rule does not distinguish between liability exclusion clauses and duty modification clauses, but instead requires disclosure of clauses which "have the effect of excluding or limiting liability for negligence". As this Report explains, such clauses will usually take the form of liability exclusion clauses. However, they can also be expressed in duty modification terms.

6.93   We have commented that it is sometimes difficult to distinguish between duty modification clauses that have the effect of excluding or limiting liability for negligence and those that do not. This is one of the major difficulties in creating a statutory scheme barring reliance on exemption clauses.

---

[42]   See Appendix C, para C.5 and following for a more general discussion of the need for regulation of charitable trusts.

[43]   See paras 2.37 to 2.38 for discussion of the use of trustee exemption clauses in charitable trusts.

[44]   Aside from policy considerations, such a requirement would be extremely onerous: see para 6.28 and following.

6.94   We believe that there are a number of reasons why similar concerns should not undermine the operation of our proposed rule of practice.

6.95   The principal object of including duty modification clauses within the scope of regulation was to ensure that any statutory prohibition of reliance on liability exclusion clauses could not be circumvented by the use of duty modification clauses which had similar effect. It was, in other words, an anti-avoidance measure.

6.96   We do not believe that the introduction of a rule of practice is likely to provoke great efforts at avoidance. Nevertheless, we do not think that it would be sensible to ignore the possible use of general standard of care modification[45] as an easy alternative to liability exclusion clauses. The formulation "a clause…which has the effect of excluding or limiting liability" would bring general standard of care modification provisions within the scope of regulation.

6.97   Of course, the intentional use of duty modification provisions as an avoidance mechanism is only part of the question. As has been explained,[46] some commonly used duty modification provisions contain an element of liability exclusion and so would fall to be disclosed under the draft rule.

6.98   In many cases, the fact that a duty modification clause engaged the rule would be obvious; for example, where the relevant provision excluded liability expressly. In other cases, the effect of the clause might be less apparent. We have outlined how some duty modification formulations could be interpreted as having the technical effect of authorising the trustee to act negligently. We have explained why we think the better view is that the majority of these clauses do not protect the trustee from negligence and so would fall outside the rule, but that the matter is not beyond dispute and that there may be cases that are particularly difficult because of the language employed.

6.99   We believe that the formulation employed by our rule will not cause difficulties in practice. This is because of the means of compliance with the rule and, especially, the mechanism of enforcement.

THE MEANS OF COMPLIANCE

6.100   We envisage that it will be relatively straightforward for trustees to comply with their obligations under the rule. In the event that a trustee is unsure of the precise technical effect of a clause it is open to the trustee to disclose the clause and its possible effect. As the rule does not (either explicitly or indirectly as a result of the consequences of non-compliance) require onerous formalities (such as independent advice), making such disclosure would not be unduly difficult.

THE MECHANISM OF ENFORCEMENT

6.101   As Part 5 has explained, we were concerned that the application of any statutory regulation of duty modification provisions would be undertaken on a highly technical basis by the court. A trustee who in good faith believed a clause to be

---

[45]   See para 5.53.

[46]   See para 5.77 and following and Appendix D.

outside the scope of regulation could be entirely undone by an adverse judicial finding. The same would be true of a regulated clause not disclosed under a statutory scheme of the sort considered earlier in this Part.

6.102 The rule of practice would not be enforced in the same way. A body regulating compliance with the rule would be unlikely to be interested in a technical error in disclosure where the trustee had acted in good faith. It would, however, be able to look through the obvious dressing-up of an exemption clause to take account of its real meaning and effect. We are confident that the rule would be applied sensitively with a view to ensuring compliance with the aims of regulation.

Transitional and jurisdictional considerations

Jurisdiction

6.103 The CP provisionally proposed that:

> ... any regulation of trustee exemption clauses should be made applicable not only to trusts governed by English law but also to persons carrying on a trust business in England and Wales.[47]

6.104 A number of consultees were critical of this proposal. Some were concerned about the potential for different treatment of co-trustees where one trustee carried on a trust business in England and Wales and another did not. Others considered the expression "carrying on a trust business in England and Wales" vague and liable to give rise to difficulties of interpretation.

6.105 One group of consultees suggested that the CP had overstated the likelihood of English settlors choosing a foreign law merely to avoid trustee exemption clause regulation and that there was no need to extend regulation to "persons carrying on a trust business in England and Wales". Another group considered the real danger to lie in regulating all English law trusts as this would impact on the current popularity of English law amongst overseas trustees and settlors and so damage the UK's invisible exports.

6.106 This is not an exhaustive list of consultees' objections. However, we see little purpose in a comprehensive discussion of the arguments for and against the CP's provisional approach in this Report as we no longer support wide-ranging statutory reform. Our recommendation that there should be a rule of practice in many ways simplifies this aspect of reform.

6.107 While we would be pleased to see the rule adopted by multi-jurisdictional and overseas regulators and professional bodies,[48] we believe that primary efforts should be aimed at ensuring the widest possible application in England and Wales.

6.108 We nevertheless recommend our rule as a matter of good practice to overseas individuals and companies who draft trusts or act as paid trustees.

[47] CP, para 4.99. See CP, para 4.98, for the reasoning behind this provisional view.

[48] STEP is a multi-jurisdictional organisation and, while its rule has so far only been approved by its England and Wales region, STEP is conducting a consultation to bring about its implementation in other regions.

6.109 We think it likely that overseas individuals and companies who draft trusts or act as paid trustees may decide to operate in accordance with the rule. Some may do so on the basis that the rule has become market standard in the English trust industry. Others may comply because they employ English professionals who are bound to take reasonable steps to ensure settlor awareness when drafting trusts. In any event, where a settlor in England or Wales is dealing with an offshore trustee, the settlor may have independent legal advice, in which case the rule can be satisfied without disclosure by the trustee.

Transitional provisions

6.110 The CP provisionally proposed that:

> … any legislative reform of trustee exemption clauses should apply to any breaches of trust which occur on or after the date when the legislation comes into force but that it should not apply to breaches of trust which precede that date.[49]

6.111 Reaction to this proposal was evenly split between those who agreed that all trustees should be made liable for negligence committed after new legislation takes effect and those who considered it unfair to impose a new regime on existing trustees. Much of the argument centred around whether or not it was appropriate or realistic to expect trustees not content to act under the new regime to retire.

6.112 Again, however, these considerations are irrelevant to our recommended model of reform. As our recommended rule governs the conduct of trustees on the setting up of a trust, it is clearly of no application to existing trusts. Trustees of existing trusts will not be expected to do anything as a result of the introduction of the rule. The rule is meaningless in such circumstances, as the settlor has already created the trust and the exemption clause; making the settlor understand the meaning and effect of such clauses would therefore have no purpose.[50]

6.113 The rule will therefore only be relevant to the creation of new trusts. Individual trustees will only be bound as soon as the rule is adopted by their regulatory bodies. However, we would urge all trustees, regulated and unregulated, to start following the requirements of the rule immediately on publication of this Report as a matter of good practice.

SPREADING BEST PRACTICE

6.114 We believe that our recommendations for implementation will give rise to regulation that will influence the vast majority of trustees.

Direct and indirect effects

6.115 The rule will directly regulate trustees who are subject to any body that either creates a bespoke rule of practice or adopts our statement of the rule. Our statement of the rule and other bodies' rules will also provide unregulated

---

[49] CP, para 4.101 (which also sets out the reasoning behind this provisional view).

trustees with a form of regulation to which they may choose to subject themselves. Voluntary compliance with any statement of the rule would offer such trustees a marketing opportunity as it would indicate compliance with best practice.

6.116   There will also be more indirect effects. The majority of trust companies and firms providing trust services will employ regulated individuals. Such individuals may, depending on the terms of the regulation binding them, be obliged to comply with the rule when drawing up trust instruments. Where this is the case, it seems likely that the organisations would themselves adopt good practice in due course.

6.117   We anticipate that best practice will seep into the consciousness of the trust industry and that standard procedure will develop in line with the rule. Such developments will be assisted by references to the rule in trust precedents and other guidance.[51] There is growing competition within the trust market. It is unlikely that a trustee would be eager to risk the potential damage to its reputation that would be associated with an outright refusal to comply with the rule. This would increasingly become the case once the bulk of the trust industry followed our recommended practice and it became the expectation that trustees adhere to the rule.

Effectiveness of the rule

6.118   It may be argued that our recommended approach suffers the defect that it only gives rise to binding obligations on the types of trustee who are most likely to act in compliance with it[52] and that it could have less impact on the least reputable elements of the trust industry.

6.119   We are aware that our proposed rule matches existing best practice. Many regulated professionals taking on the role of trustee routinely point out exemption provisions to their clients, and explain their purpose and effect. They view this simply as an aspect of proper conduct and do not need a rule to tell them what to do.

6.120   The fact that some regulated trustees already adopt good practice cannot, however, form the basis of a principled objection to a rule requiring all regulated trustees to act in a similarly proper fashion. We do not envisage that the rule would be onerous for those who already act in accordance with good practice.[53] It would, however, play an important educational role in relation to regulated practitioners who are less expert in trust matters. It would also be of substantive use in the rare cases of determined improper practice. Where a regulated professional could be shown not to have followed good practice, he or she would be liable to meaningful sanctions. The rule would consequently protect those who

---

[50]   In many cases the settlor will not even be alive.

[51]   For example, STEP publishes its own recommended standard trust clauses which are highly influential on the practice of its members and other practitioners.

[52]   Expert professionals and those achieving membership of prestigious trade associations.

[53]   Provided they did not take disproportionate steps to ensure compliance.

follow best practice from the activities of those liable to bring their profession into disrepute.

6.121 We are also unconvinced by the argument that it is inappropriate to introduce reform unless it can bite on all trustees. Notwithstanding our belief that most unregulated trustees would be influenced by the rule, it may well be the case that some trustees would continue to rely on "hidden" exemption clauses. That group might indeed include some of the less reputable trustees.

6.122 We cannot, however, accept that the fact that the rule will not bind all trustees is a good reason for abandoning our recommendation. One needs to consider the alternatives. We could, in the light of the acknowledged difficulty of creating comprehensive non-statutory regulation, revert to our initial plans for wide legislative reform. However, we have shown how a statutory scheme capable of catching the worst offenders would give rise to significant difficulties. The other alternative is to do nothing. The industry must ask itself whether it really would prefer to lose the opportunity to improve the protections offered to settlors merely because those protections may not be effective in all cases. For us the answer is obvious: the fact that the rule would not bind trustees in all cases should not mean that there should be no rule at all.

6.123 We should finally point out that the extent of regulation is not fixed. The initial application of the rule is simply a reflection of the current regulatory system. The reason why we are able to push for the adoption of the rule by solicitors and not by, for example, will writers is that the former have been considered suitable for regulation while the latter, so far, have not. In the event that will writers were regulated, it would be appropriate for our proposed rule to bind them in the same way as solicitors. Indeed, it is possible that evidence of widespread failure by a particular type of trustee to adopt the rule of practice could provide an additional basis for their regulation.

6.124 It appears that in the relatively near future there will be comprehensive trust regulation (of some sort) in the UK. The Third Money Laundering Directive[54] requires Member States to provide that "trust and company service providers"[55] must be licensed or registered in order to operate their business legally.[56] A body given the function of licensing or registration for this purpose by a Member State must refuse licensing or registration to a trust or company service provider if it is not satisfied that the persons who control the provider[57] are fit and proper persons.[58]

---

[54] Third Money Laundering Directive 2005/60/EC (OJ L309 25.11.2005 p 15).

[55] Third Money Laundering Directive, 2005/60/EC (OJ L309 25.11.2005 p 15), art 3(7) defines "trust and company service providers" as any natural or legal person which by way of business provides any of the specified services to third parties. These services include "acting as or arranging for another person to act as a trustee of an express trust or a similar legal arrangement".

[56] Third Money Laundering Directive, 2005/60/EC (OJ L309 25.11.2005 p 15), art 36(1).

[57] Third Money Laundering Directive, 2005/60/EC (OJ L309 25.11.2005 p 15), art 36(2), refers to "the persons who effectively direct or will direct the business of such entities or the beneficial owners of such entities".

[58] Third Money Laundering Directive, 2005/60/EC (OJ L309 25.11.2005 p 15), art 36(2).

6.125 Ensuring compliance with our proposed rule could be added to the functions of the body or bodies responsible for trust service provider registration or licensing for the purposes of the Directive.[59] Whether or not Government considers it appropriate to have compliance with our proposed rule enforced by the registration or licensing body (or bodies) may depend on the voluntary uptake of the rule within the trust industry.

---

[59] This would require primary legislation, and could not be accomplished through regulations made under the European Communities Act 1972, s 2, to implement the Directive.

PART 7
SUMMARY OF RECOMMENDATIONS

7.1   We recommend that a rule of practice should be recognised in the interests of securing settlor awareness of trustee exemption clauses.

7.2   We recommend that the main elements of the rule should be as follows:

> Any paid trustee who causes a settlor to include a clause in a trust instrument which has the effect of excluding or limiting liability for negligence must before the creation of the trust take such steps as are reasonable to ensure that the settlor is aware of the meaning and effect of the clause.

7.3   We recommend that regulatory and professional bodies should make regulation to such effect in order to meet the particular circumstances of their membership and should enforce such regulation in accordance with their codes of conduct. Bodies whose membership includes the drafters of trusts should extend regulation to those who draft trust documentation containing trustee exemption provisions.

7.4   We recommend that Government should promote the application of this rule of practice as widely as possible across the trust industry.

APPENDIX A
REFORM OPTIONS CONSIDERED AND REJECTED IN THE CONSULTATION PAPER

A.1 Having established that there should be some regulation of trustee exemption clauses and that this should apply only to a particular class of trustee, the CP considered a number of possible approaches to regulation. This Appendix considers the alternative approaches rejected by the CP, namely to:

> (1) impose an absolute prohibition on reliance on trustee exemption clauses;

> (2) impose a reasonableness requirement such that professional trustees are only permitted to rely upon a trustee exemption clause in so far as the clause satisfies the requirement of reasonableness;

> (3) prohibit professional trustees from relying on trustee exemption clauses but permitting them to apply for exculpatory relief from the court; and

> (4) allow limited effect to trustee exemption clauses where there is a professional trustee but restricting their effectiveness once the conduct of the trustee crosses a certain threshold.

A.2 With due respect to those who argued in favour of these regulatory approaches, we do not attempt a comprehensive analysis of every option. Consultation confirmed our provisional view that none of the alternatives rejected in the CP offers an appropriate model for reform, in most cases on the grounds set out in the CP.

ALTERNATIVE MODEL 1: ABSOLUTE PROHIBITION

A.3 The CP took the provisional view that:

> We do not consider that an outright prohibition of trustee exemption clauses is justified or necessary.[1]

A.4 An absolute prohibition of trustee exemption clauses would result in trustees being liable for all breaches of trust, whether negligent or not. It would have the practical effect of imposing strict personal liability on all trustees irrespective of the circumstances surrounding the particular trust and the specific wishes of the settlor.

A.5 The CP argued that to deny settlors all power to modify or to restrict the liabilities of the trustee would inevitably cause trusts to become less flexible. Outright prohibition would be likely to have an undesirable effect on the provision of trust services, deterring many of those who are at present willing to take up the duties of trusteeship. It suggested that other means of trustee protection, centrally the power to apply to court to be excused from liability for breach of trust,[2] do not

---

[1] CP, para 4.19.

[2] Trustee Act 1925, s 61.

provide a satisfactory alternative, as the outcomes of such applications are uncertain.[3]

The reaction on consultation

A.6 The vast majority of consultees agreed with our provisional view that there should be no outright prohibition of trustee exemption clauses.

A.7 Some pointed to the importance of trustee exemption clauses in particular circumstances, such as where there is a history of conflict between potential beneficiaries. Others referred to established practices in specific markets. Many respondents reinforced the CP's comment that complete legislative prohibition would destroy the flexibility inherent in trusts.

Conclusion

A.8 There was little support for the outright prohibition of trustee exemption clauses.

ALTERNATIVE MODEL 2: A REASONABLENESS REQUIREMENT

A.9 The CP invited views on the possible statutory regulation of trustee exemption clauses by means of a rule that

> … a clause can only be relied upon by a trustee to exclude or restrict his or her liability for breach of trust in so far as the clause satisfies a requirement of reasonableness.[4]

A.10 The CP pointed out that this type of approach, focusing on the terms of the trust, is similar to that employed by the Unfair Contract Terms Act 1977. It would, the CP argued, "have the benefits of flexibility, sophistication and adaptability to the circumstances of each trust".[5] Over time, the courts would develop guidance as to which clauses are likely to be upheld and which are likely to be struck down. Trustees would be deterred from employing the types of clauses that had been established as excessively wide. The long-term effect could therefore be to modify standard trust terms so as to ensure compliance with the statutory requirements.[6]

A.11 However, the CP provisionally rejected this approach to regulation. It questioned whether it was right to confine the application of the test to the circumstances prevailing at the date of the execution of the trust. As the identity of trustees and beneficiaries is likely to change over time, it could be inappropriate to ask whether a trustee exemption clause is reasonable without any reference to the trustee's conduct.[7]

A.12 The CP noted the transitional difficulties associated with such an approach. If a reasonableness requirement were applied to all trusts (irrespective of their date

---

[3] See CP, 4.18 to 4.19.

[4] CP, para 4.52.

[5] CP, para 4.47.

[6] See CP, para 4.40 to 4.49.

[7] CP, para 4.50.

of execution) the trustees of many existing trusts would become vulnerable to attack and might become disinclined to continue to act.[8]

The reaction on consultation

A.13 The majority of consultees concurred with the arguments put forward in the CP.

A.14 Many of those who disagreed and considered a reasonableness test desirable did so on grounds of consistency. They thought that similar tests should be applied to trustee exemption clauses and contractual exemption clauses. The consistency argument was applied most strongly in relation to commercial trusts. Consultees considered such trusts to be performing a similar economic function to contracts (especially where beneficiaries have contributed to the trust fund) and suggested that differences of treatment should be eliminated.

A.15 A number of consultees laid emphasis on the CP's acknowledgement that a test of reasonableness would enable the courts to take a flexible approach to regulation and could be easily applied to different types of trustee.

A.16 However, most consultees were concerned about the difficulties that a requirement of reasonableness might cause in practice. Many were clear that the test would give rise to considerable uncertainty and litigation, especially in the short term. It would be unclear how reasonableness would be judged, especially as courts would work with the benefit of hindsight.

A.17 A number of consultees suggested that the mere possibility of retrospective challenge would lead to difficulties. On the one hand, it could be argued that no trustee should need to know in advance whether or not they can rely on a clause excusing them for negligence as their intention should be to act properly. However, it is not unreasonable for a trustee to want to know the extent of its protection before deciding whether or not to take on a trusteeship and when setting the level of its fees. An indemnity insurer would also want certainty as to the protections available to a trustee before setting the level of premium.

A.18 Regulation of this sort would place trustees in an invidious position as regards clauses authorising the trustee to take or not to take a particular action and exempting them from any consequent liability. The trustee would have no means of knowing whether compliance with the express wishes of the settlor could lead to liability at a future date.

Conclusion

A.19 We stand by the position taken in the CP that a reasonableness requirement is not the best means of regulating reliance on trustee exemption clauses. As consultees made clear, the uncertainty that such a requirement would introduce would undermine trustees' ability to act decisively in the interests of the beneficiaries and would lead to an increase in litigation. As the discussion of a reasonableness test (albeit in a different context) at paragraph 5.63 and following indicates, such uncertainty would also be likely to diminish the flexibility inherent in the trust concept and in some cases undermine the viability of the whole trust.

---

[8]   CP, para 4.51.

ALTERNATIVE MODEL 3: EXCULPATORY RELIEF

A.20   The CP considered and rejected regulation of the sort recommended by the New Zealand Law Commission:

> We do not consider it satisfactory to combine an outright prohibition of trustee exemption clauses with the exercise of a judicial discretion to exculpate trustees who have acted honestly and reasonably and who ought fairly to be excused for their breach of trust.[9]

A.21   The CP noted that section 61 of the Trustee Act 1925 already gives the court a discretion to relieve trustees from personal liability for breach of trust where they have acted "honestly and reasonably, and ought fairly to be excused". However, it acknowledged that courts in England and Wales have been reluctant to exercise that discretion in favour of trustees. Relief under the section appears to be limited to cases of honest mistake made where there has been no element of carelessness in the trustee's conduct.[10]

A.22   The CP noted that "professional trustees are not treated generously"[11] under the current exculpatory jurisdiction and surmised that: "unless there is a change of culture among the judiciary towards applications under section 61, professional trustees are unlikely to consider its invocation as a satisfactory alternative to the use of trustee exemption clauses".[12] It follows that if professional trustees were denied reliance on exemption clauses and forced instead to seek exculpation, section 61 would not be an adequate vehicle for such relief.

A.23   The CP raised a second objection to the New Zealand approach: that it requires litigation to discover whether liability is to be incurred by the trustee. This, it suggested, would not be conducive to certainty or predictability.[13]

The reaction on consultation

A.24   A strong majority of respondents agreed with the Law Commission's provisional view. Most did so on the basis that a judicial discretion to exculpate trustees would lead to litigation. It would require trustees who had acted properly to undergo the court process in order to gain exculpation, a costly exercise, and it would make any claim by beneficiaries subject to an uncertain defence.

A.25   Consultees were also concerned that a provision of this type would cause trustees to be more cautious, seeking directions before making decisions (the costs of which would be borne by the trust fund).

A.26   Consultees concurred with the CP's view that the courts have been reluctant to take advantage of the existing section 61 power to relieve trustees (especially professionals) from personal liability for breach of trust. Many were consequently

---

[9]   CP, para 4.66.

[10] CP, para 4.63.

[11] CP, para 4.63.

[12] CP, paras 4.63 and 4.64.

[13] CP, para 4.65.

sceptical that the courts would be willing to exercise any new power to exculpate paid trustees who had committed a breach of trust.

A.27 A few consultees were more receptive to a New Zealand-type approach. The Law Reform Committee of the Bar Council suggested that "the exculpation provision could be so worded...that the judiciary would be bound to interpret it appropriately" and considered this model to be a more flexible approach than merely looking at the nature of the breach. One consultee[14] found the model "attractive because it maximises prophylaxis by creating a bright-line rule yet softens the operation of the rule by discretion in extreme cases. ... Such an approach has good equitable precedents, as in self-dealing and profit-taking by a fiduciary, where a generous discretionary allowance is given back to a deserving fiduciary who has been stripped of profits".

Conclusion

A.28 Although a small number of consultees argued eloquently in favour of an exculpatory relief approach, we are not persuaded. Any regulation which gives rise to uncertainty and litigation is helpful to neither trustees nor beneficiaries.

ALTERNATIVE MODEL 4: LIMITING THE EFFECTIVENESS OF EXEMPTION CLAUSES

A.29 The final general approach to regulation considered in the CP would operate by allowing limited effect to trustee exemption clauses but restricting their effectiveness once the conduct of the trustee crossed a certain threshold. Like the exculpatory relief model, all the variations of this model therefore concentrate on the conduct of the trustee rather than the terminology of the exemption clause.

A.30 The CP considered a number of possible thresholds:[15]

(1) where the trustee's conduct has been so unreasonable, irresponsible or incompetent that it should not be capable of being excused;

(2) where it is unreasonable for the trustee to escape liability by reference to all the circumstances including the nature and extent of the breach of trust itself; and

(3) where the trustee has been grossly negligent.

Proposed threshold (1) – conduct too unreasonable, irresponsible or incompetent

A.31 We invited views on regulation providing that:

... professional trustees should be unable to rely upon a trustee exemption clause where their conduct has been so unreasonable,

---

[14] Dr Joshua Getzler, Fellow and Tutor in Law, St Hugh's College, Oxford.

[15] A fourth threshold – negligence – has been considered in Part 5.

irresponsible or incompetent that in fairness to the beneficiary the trustee should not be excused.[16]

A.32   The CP[17] based this model on one of several options proposed by the British Columbia Law Institute.[18] Under the model, trustee exemption clauses would be *prima facie* effective, according to their terms, to relieve a trustee of liability for breach of trust. However, in the event of a breach, it would be open to a beneficiary to apply to the court for a declaration that the exemption clause was ineffective in relation to that breach. The penalty for excessively unreasonable, irresponsible or incompetent conduct would be that the trustee would be unable to rely on the clause, and the trustee's liability would be determined as if the clause was not contained in the trust instrument.

A.33   This model was suggested as an alternative to a rule preventing exemption in respect of gross negligence. It would have the effect of denying paid trustees resort to an exclusion clause where they have committed a particularly serious breach of trust.[19]

The reaction on consultation

A.34   As expected, very few consultees approved of this approach to regulation.

A.35   Those who found this alternative attractive generally did so because of the flexibility it affords in determining whether trustees ought to incur liability for particular breaches of trust. They considered that this test would best allow justice to be done to trustees and beneficiaries. A few consultees suggested a further refinement to the test: that the burden of proof should be borne by defaulting trustees so that they would be excused only where they could show that their conduct has been reasonable, responsible and competent.

A.36   However, the majority of consultees rejected this formulation, arguing that its operation would be vague, especially until case law guidance had developed. Consultees argued that, by its very nature, retrospectivity would lead to uncertainty for trustees and to unfair results. As the test relies on the concept of reasonableness (albeit expressed negatively) it suffers from the various drawbacks discussed when considering Alternative Model 2 above.

Conclusion

A.37   We see nothing in the consultation responses to alter our initial view that this is not a sensible way to proceed.

---

[16]   CP, para 4.78.

[17]   At para 4.58 and following.

[18]   British Columbia Law Institute, *Report on Exculpation Clauses in Trust Instruments* (March 2002) BCLI Report No 17, available at http://www.bcli.org/pages/projects/trustee/ExculpationClauses.html (last visited 16 June 2006).

[19]   CP, para 4.78.

Proposed threshold (2) – unreasonable to escape liability in all the circumstances

A.38 The CP invited views as to:

> … whether professional trustees should not be able to exclude liability for breach of trust where it is not reasonable for the trustees to rely upon a trustee exemption clause contained in the trust instrument by reference to all the circumstances including the nature and extent of the breach of trust itself.[20]

A.39 The CP suggested, immediately after provisionally proposing its preferred form of regulation,[21] that it would be useful to explore the level of support for this variant of the limited effectiveness model. This approach would allow the court to take account of the nature of the trust, the type of trustee and all other circumstances. It would therefore confer considerable flexibility in determining whether trustees should be rendered fully accountable for their conduct or should be able to invoke the protection of an exemption clause.[22]

The reaction on consultation

A.40 There was little support for this form of regulation.

A.41 Some consultees approved of the flexibility it would allow in determining whether a trustee should incur liability. However, most disliked the formulation on the grounds that it would give rise to uncertainty and litigation. The position would not become significantly clearer with the emergence of judicial guidance as litigation would be decided on the precise facts of each case.

Conclusion

A.42 We support the CP's provisional view that this type of test would not be an appropriate or workable basis for regulation.

Proposed threshold (3) – gross negligence

A.43 The CP stated that:

> We do not consider that the concept of gross negligence is sufficiently clear or distinctive as to form the basis of regulation of trustee exemption clauses. We do not therefore propose that those who wish to claim for breach of trust should be obliged to establish that the trustees were guilty of gross negligence in order to deny them resort to any exemption clause in the trust instrument.[23]

A.44 The CP outlined a number of possible reasons for following the example of Jersey and Guernsey.[24] Such an approach would represent a compromise

---

[20] CP, para 4.86.

[21] See Part 5.

[22] CP, para 4.86.

[23] CP, para 4.78.

[24] Both jurisdictions regulate on the basis of gross negligence: see CP, paras 4.67 to 4.78.

between (a) the ability under the current law to exclude liability for any honest action or omission, and (b) a proposal to prohibit reliance on clauses excluding liability for any act of negligence. It would have the advantage of protecting beneficiaries' financial interests from the consequences of the most objectionable instances of trustee negligence, without stripping trustees of all protection. It would respect, to some degree, the autonomy of settlors.[25]

A.45 However, the CP concluded that an approach of this sort would be unworkable without a clear distinction between gross and ordinary negligence.[26] The meaning of "gross negligence" in English law is not sufficiently clear for courts to be able to establish whether a trustee's conduct in any particular case has crossed the border from the merely negligent to the grossly negligent. The adoption of this distinction as the basis for regulation of trustee exemption clauses could therefore generate uncertainty and litigation.[27]

The reaction on consultation

A.46 The vast majority of consultees agreed with the provisional view. Most did so on the basis that gross negligence is an alien concept to English law which, if introduced, would give rise to confusion. Although gross negligence has been recognised by the English courts when considering other areas of law,[28] it was generally felt that its introduction in the context of trustee exemption clauses would be inappropriate.

A.47 A small number of consultees disagreed, arguing that a court would be able to distinguish satisfactorily between gross and ordinary negligence in the trust context if so required. Some pointed to the current practice of referring to "gross negligence" in trust instruments as indicating a degree of confidence that, if asked, the English courts could give meaning to the term. Other consultees suggested that, even if the current law on gross negligence is unclear, legislation could clarify its meaning. The courts of Scotland and various other jurisdictions that recognise the distinction have, they argued, no real difficulty in formulating the concept.

Conclusion

A.48 The responses to the consultation question support our provisional view that the concept of "gross negligence" is unclear. We accept that the phrase could be defined in statute. We do not, however, believe that even this would remove all uncertainty, especially in the short term. Any definition would have to formulate fine distinctions which have yet to be considered in the trusts context.

---

[25] CP, para 4.67.

[26] CP, para 4.68.

[27] CP, para 4.70 and following.

[28] See CP, para 4.67 and following.

APPENDIX B
TRUSTEE INDEMNITY INSURANCE

INTRODUCTION

B.1 The issue of trustee indemnity insurance featured strongly in consultees' responses to the CP.

B.2 Some consultees concentrated on the effect of a statutory restriction of reliance on exemption provisions on the availability of indemnity insurance and the size of premiums. Many addressed the CP's specific provisional proposal in relation to trustee indemnity insurance:

> We provisionally propose that all trustees should be given power to make payments out of the trust fund to purchase indemnity insurance to cover their liability for breach of trust.[1]

B.3 The CP justified the provisional proposal on the basis that authorising trustees to finance liability insurance cover from the trust fund would be of general benefit to beneficiaries.[2] Loss would therefore be allocated between the beneficiaries of all trusts (through higher administration charges) in contrast with the current system in which the entire burden is born by those beneficiaries who suffer loss at the hands of defaulting trustees who are able to rely on exemption clauses.

B.4 Of course, while the CP's provisional proposal for a power of insurance was free-standing, it must be read in the context of the CP's provisional prohibition of reliance on clauses exempting the trustee from liability for negligence. Insurance would, in the event of this denial of protection, enable trustees to meet claims made against them, avoiding shortfalls where trustees are "men of straw". The availability of indemnity insurance would additionally encourage trustees to overcome any reluctance to act for a trust where they were unable to rely on an exemption clause.

B.5 The following paragraphs outline consultees' reaction to the CP's provisional proposal for a power of insurance against the backdrop of its proposed regulation of exemption provisions. Later in this Appendix we explain why, in the light of our other recommendations of reform, we have decided not to recommend the introduction of a statutory power to insure.

THE REACTION ON CONSULTATION

B.6 There was some support for the CP's provisional proposal that all trustees should be given power to fund the purchase of indemnity insurance from the trust fund. A number of consultees felt that the power would be particularly useful in non-standard circumstances, such as in recruiting trustees to act for "difficult" family trusts. Others suggested that the power is especially needed to protect lay

---

[1] CP, para 4.32.

[2] It would also provide unpaid trustees with the same opportunity to protect themselves as paid trustees (who are able to fund indemnity insurance indirectly from the trust fund via their fees). See CP, para 4.26 and following.

trustees. However, the majority of consultees disagreed with the provisional proposal to give all trustees a power to insure of this sort.

Objections of principle

B.7 Several consultees considered it inconsistent to prohibit trustees from protecting themselves from the consequences of their actions and omissions by means of an exemption clause while allowing them to do so by means of insurance paid for by the trust fund. In both cases the trust assets are depleted and the trustee, the party responsible for the depletion, fails to bear the cost. One consultee[3] commented that "no other profession…places the burden of insuring against its own negligence directly as an individual charge against the client's own funds…it would appear quite odious to beneficiaries that they were directly burdened with the costs of insuring against trustees' negligence".

B.8 It was also contended that the provisional proposal that trustees should be given an uncapped power to meet the cost of insurance out of the trust fund is wrong in principle as it undermines the deterrent effect of insurance premiums. A trustee who is not required to fund its own insurance is, from an insurance point of view, under no pressure to keep premiums low by acting in a way that avoids the risk of a claim.[4] While a poor claims record should affect the competitiveness of the trustee when bidding for other work, the heightened premium would not be apparent to settlors considering whether or not to appoint the trustee unless they specifically asked about the trustee's claims history. Few settlors would be sufficiently aware to do this, or to assess properly the impact of any information provided. Trustees would be likely to resist such disclosure, on grounds of client and commercial confidentiality.

B.9 Finally, a number of consultees argued that a default power of insurance would be unfair on the beneficiaries of well-run trusts whose insurance contributions would, in effect, be subsidising the beneficiaries of trusts more likely to suffer loss.[5] Why, they contended, should settlors who have taken great care in the selection of their trustees have to accept the cost of insurance to make allowance for those who funds have suffered loss through the negligence of the incompetent trustees they have selected?

Practical difficulties

B.10 In addition, consultees outlined significant practical problems with the CP's proposed power. They also commented on the likely consequences for insurance of the CP's provisionally proposed restriction of reliance on exemption clauses.

---

[3] Barclays Bank Trust Company Ltd.

[4] Though there may be a power to remove the trustee, which could be exercised either as a result of a rise in premiums following a breach (in relation to that trust or any other trust) or as a result of the breach itself.

[5] The economic effect would be broadly similar to a compulsory levy on trust beneficiaries to fund a compensation scheme intended to compensate those who have suffered loss through trustee negligence.

Cost

B.11 The CP recognised that any restriction on reliance on trustee exemption clauses was almost certain to have the side effect of increasing the cost of trustee indemnity insurance.[6] Such increases would be borne by the trust fund, either directly[7] or indirectly.[8]

B.12 It would be logical to expect the total increases in premiums roughly to match the total amounts potentially payable to make good trustee negligence. If this were the case, the overall loss to trusts should be minimal. However, consultation suggested that the reality was unlikely to be so simple and that the type of insurance cover envisaged by the CP would in fact be prohibitively expensive.

B.13 Consultees reported that trustees had recently experienced sharp increases in insurance premiums and expected continued rises in the future. Some attributed the increases in premiums to reductions in capacity in the professional indemnity insurance market and anticipated further deterioration in the market over the near and medium term. A number of responses suggested that the cost of insurance is already sufficiently high for a number of institutions to prefer to self-insure.

B.14 The majority of consultees were clear that this already difficult situation would worsen in the event that insurers were denied the indirect protection that trustee exemption clauses currently offer. They claimed that the effect of the CP's provisionally proposed regulation of exemption clauses would be to increase premiums yet further, quite possibly by amounts far exceeding the increase in risk. There could also be increases in insurance excesses.

B.15 Some consultees concentrated on the cost implications of the particular type of indemnity insurance envisaged by the proposal: stand-alone policies covering the risk of acting for individual trusts. It was suggested that insurers would have little choice but to impose high premiums on inexperienced trustees because of the difficulties of assessing the risk posed by applicants with no track record of acting as trustee.

B.16 However, consultees did not consider that the problem would be limited to inexperienced trustees. Consultees suggested that premiums payable for such insurance would be significantly higher than the indirect cost of professional trustees' general indemnity insurance, passed on as part of the trustees' fees. Of course, the availability of a power to take out insurance would not force those trustees who currently insure themselves as a business to take out separate cover for individual trusts. However, the temptation would be to do so, as it would allow trustees to offer a lower up-front fee.

B.17 Another concern about the cost effectiveness of the provisional proposal related to the dynamic of taking out insurance. The Chancery Bar Association commented in its response that "it is a fact of business life that if the person

---

[6] See CP, para 4.26.

[7] Where the trust instrument authorises indemnity insurance premiums to be paid out of the trust fund.

[8] Where paid trustees pass on the cost of indemnity insurance to the trust in their administration fees.

negotiating the amount to be paid for something is not the person actually bearing the cost of it, it has an inflationary effect on the amounts involved".[9]

B.18 Consultees pointed to other inflationary pressures. Some considered that as top-level trust corporations and professional trustees are already insured, the new applicants for insurance would be likely to be drawn from smaller, less experienced firms, with less sophisticated risk management systems and less proven track records. Others predicted that as an insured trustee is considered fair game by beneficiaries, there would be little incentive to compromise or to limit the claim to a reasonable sum, as the trustee's expenses would be met by insurance.

B.19 While not all consultees agreed that the consequences would inevitably be so adverse, the majority view was extremely pessimistic.

Availability

B.20 There was a consensus among many consultees that trustee indemnity insurance might not, in practice, be as readily available as the CP supposed. A number of respondents suggested that adequate indemnity insurance is already in many cases unobtainable.

B.21 Particular circumstances can exacerbate the problem. A number of consultees pointed out the existing difficulties involved in obtaining adequate insurance for high-value trusts, such as those used in capital markets transactions. Law Debenture Trust Corporation Plc reported that in their experience "there is simply no appetite for insurers to assume transaction specific risk on innovative transactions".

B.22 Increased risk can also be an issue in non-commercial trusts. It was claimed that it is virtually impossible for a family member to obtain insurance in respect of a family trust, as family disputes can be extremely difficult.

B.23 Other consultees contended that the stand-alone policies envisaged in the CP are currently not easy to obtain and that the market lacks capacity to offer such products. They argued that insurers rarely write policies relating to individual trusts; most trustees take out professional indemnity insurance covering all their work as trustees or all the professional services they offer. Professional trustees are therefore insured on the basis of a spread of risk over the entirety of the portfolio that they manage.

B.24 This has obvious implications for trustees acting otherwise than in business, especially unpaid trustees. STEP suggested that "it would be…extremely difficult to obtain specific insurance for professional trustees acting gratuitously or by reference to one specific engagement". The suggestion that trustees take out a series of individual policies rather than a blanket policy covering all trust business could, therefore, not just be expensive; it could be impossible to achieve.

---

[9] For example, it has been suggested that poor value for money may be obtained in the context of insurance connected with conditional fee agreements. Insurance is taken out by solicitors on behalf of their clients to cover the defendant's costs in the event of their clients' legal action being unsuccessful.

B.25   An alternative course might be to allow professional trustees to continue to be insured on a whole-business basis and to provide a trustee power to allocate the premium between the individual trusts. However, this begs the question of how part of a premium could attributed to any particular trust; the insurer will not have considered the risk posed by that trust and so the trustee will not be in a position to assess what would be a fair allocation.

B.26   Finally, respondents raised a number of technical issues about the adequacy of current cover. Some pointed out that many trustees who are professionals currently rely on the negligence cover provided by their partnership or business. This may or may not cover all breach of trust claims, especially where the trustee is acting pro bono. Others noted the effect of the delay between work done as a trustee and claims in respect of that work; it could be many years before any loss becomes apparent. Insurance cover will often not extend this far.[10]

Meeting the premiums

B.27   Several consultees criticised the suggestion that trustees meet premiums out of the trust fund on the basis that sufficient liquid funds will not always be available. How would the proposal assist where the trust does not generate cash; for example, a trust of private company shares which do not pay dividends? The trustees could generate cash by the sale of trust assets, but this would often go against the underlying purpose of the trust. Similar problems would be faced by trustees of financial market trusts and pension funds where there is no unallocated pool of funds from which the trustee could reimburse itself for the cost of insurance.[11]

B.28   A further complication arises where the trust's only asset is cash on income account; expending this on premiums would mean that the income account bore the whole of the brunt of the cost of insurance, even though some of the benefit would be enjoyed by the capital beneficiaries.

Assessment of consultees' concerns

B.29   Consultation therefore highlighted a range of concerns about the CP's provisional proposal for a power to fund indemnity insurance, and about the possible effects of the CP's proposed regulation of exemption clauses on such insurance.

B.30   We are aware that those who opposed the CP's provisional proposals for the regulation of trustee exemption clauses had an interest in putting forward such arguments. Nonetheless, the extent of opposition to the suggestions made in the CP have forced us to reconsider our policy.

B.31   While we see the force of consultees' principled concerns about the CP's proposed power to insure, we feel that in many cases the contrary argument can be made. For example, we do not accept that it is necessarily the fault of beneficiaries that their trustees administer funds less effectively than others (any

[10]   Insurance may be written so as to cover claims notified during the insured period rather than the events giving rise to loss.

[11]   In other types of capital markets transactions such as securitisations, cash may be available but the credit rating of the transaction will be based upon unimpeded income streams and fixed levels of expenditure throughout the life of the transaction.

more than it is to the credit of other beneficiaries that they have capable and effective trustees). It could also be argued that trustees are in a much better position efficiently to bear the cost of their own negligence than are beneficiaries. It would seem that there are economies of both scale and scope that would make it cheaper for paid trustees to obtain indemnity insurance than for beneficiaries to obtain first party insurance against the risk of third party professional negligence. If it is not economically viable for beneficiaries to insure against their potential losses, the only means of achieving this benefit for beneficiaries may be to permit trustees to insure.

B.32   It is impossible to predict precisely how the insurance market would react to the regulation of trustee exemption clauses and the introduction of a default power of insurance. The uncertainty is exacerbated by the fact that there is not a single type of trustee indemnity insurance available. Rather, bespoke insurance is (albeit perhaps rarely) offered in respect of individual trusts, the risks in respect of such policies being sensitively fact-specific, and all-business insurance is written to professionals based on their overall activities.

B.33   However, we are persuaded by the responses of consultees that there is a significant risk that the cost of the type of insurance envisaged by the CP would be high, quite possibly out of proportion to the protection it would offer. We accept that it is not in the interests of beneficiaries to enrich the insurance industry at the expense of trust funds. As premiums would be taken from the trust fund after the trust had been established, the true cost would not be obvious to the settlor.

B.34   The likely availability of trustee insurance is also difficult to predict. There is a clear incentive to insurers to write business. However, we do accept that the cost to insurers of assessing the risk, particularly of smaller trusts, may make the business unattractive. With higher-risk trusts the potential for loss could deter insurers altogether.

B.35   As trusts are themselves so diverse, it would be simplistic to consider there to be a single market for trustee indemnity insurance. The particular market conditions, and the factors which would determine the availability and cost of indemnity insurance, vary widely.

Family trusts

B.36   We have seen evidence that a default power of insurance would be difficult to translate into the family trust context. Most paid trustees are professional advisers, who currently rely on general professional indemnity insurance, which should include cover for their work as trustees. Given the idiosyncrasies of family arrangements, stand-alone policies could be expensive to write, particularly for lay trustees.

Commercial trusts

B.37   Most trustees of commercial trusts appear to rely on general professional indemnity cover to provide some degree of indemnity insurance for their trusts work. Consultees emphasised the huge potential liability in commercial trust cases and doubted whether insurers would be willing to assume the risk of insuring specific transactions for large sums, with the possibility of such losses.

Furthermore, there does not appear to be any real expectation in the market that financial market trustees would have sufficient assets or insurance cover to meet a breach of trust claim.

Pension trusts

B.38 Different considerations apply again in the pension trust world where trustees operate in an established market. Although the potential exposure to liability is high, the obligations of pension trustees are fairly standard across the market, and most pension trustees are professionals, which may be seen to reduce the risk of incurring liability. In the case of occupational pensions, the employer will generally indemnify the trustees in the last resort, which may limit the amount of insurance cover required.

Charitable trusts

B.39 Specific considerations most obviously apply to charities. Clause 39 of the Charities Bill will insert into the Charities Act 1993 a default power to purchase indemnity insurance:

"73F Trustees' indemnity insurance

(1)   The charity trustees of a charity may arrange for the purchase, out of the funds of the charity, of insurance designed to indemnify the charity trustees or any trustees for the charity against any personal liability in respect of—

(a)   any breach of trust or breach of duty committed by them in their capacity as charity trustees or trustees for the charity, or

(b)   any negligence, default, breach of duty or breach of trust committed by them in their capacity as directors or officers of the charity (if it is a body corporate) or of any body corporate carrying on any activities on behalf of the charity.

(2)   The terms of such insurance must, however, be so framed as to exclude the provision of any indemnity for a person in respect of—

(a)   any liability incurred by him to pay—

(i)   a fine imposed in criminal proceedings, or

(ii)   a sum payable to a regulatory authority by way of a penalty in respect of non-compliance with any requirement of a regulatory nature (however arising);

(b)   any liability incurred by him in defending any criminal proceedings in which he is convicted of an offence arising out of any fraud or dishonesty, or wilful or reckless misconduct, by him; or

(c)   any liability incurred by him to the charity that arises out of any conduct which he knew (or must reasonably be assumed to have known) was not in the interests of the charity or in the case of which he did not care.

B.40 The default power is therefore subject to limitations[12] and contains safeguards against inappropriate use by requiring the trustees to take appropriate care when making the decision to purchase insurance[13] and by imposing an overriding duty to act in the best interests of the charity.[14]

B.41 We see a number of reasons why the introduction of such a power is unlikely to give rise to the types of problems identified by responses to our consultation.

B.42 As paid charity trustees can already obtain insurance and factor the cost of it into their fees, the default power is of particular value to unpaid trustees. The unpaid trustees of charitable trusts are, compared to other trustees, unlikely to be found liable for breach of trust. Charitable trusts have no individual beneficiaries, who in the private trust context may be quick to litigate to protect their interests. The Charity Commission, acting for the Attorney-General, is able to instigate proceedings against charity trustees, but it is uncommon for it to do so against unpaid trustees in the absence of dishonesty.[15] It normally takes legal action only where there is evidence of bad faith or serious mismanagement, as it does not wish to discourage volunteers from acting as trustees. The courts, in turn, tend to exhibit a level of sympathy to charity trustees.

B.43 The risk to the unpaid trustees' indemnity insurers is therefore relatively low. There is consequently less reason to believe that insurance will not continue to be available at a reasonable price in consequence of the conferral of the power in the Charities Bill.

Conclusions

B.44 There is no doubt that the issue of trustee indemnity insurance is much more complicated than presented in the CP. It is now clear that there can be no guarantee that the type of insurance described in the CP would be obtainable (especially by inexperienced trustees), whether or not trustee exemption clauses were regulated in the manner provisionally proposed in the CP. We accept that even where insurance remained available, cover might be prohibitively expensive.

B.45 The evidence therefore suggests that a universal power for trustees to insure themselves at the cost of the trust fund would be of limited utility. Arguably, the need for such a power is also reduced by our rejection of the CP's provisional proposal restricting reliance on trustee exemption clauses. Should, however, the power nevertheless be made available so that it can be used where circumstances allow?

---

[12] In the proposed s 73F(2).

[13] Proposed s 73F(5).

[14] Proposed s 73F(4).

[15] The Charities Bill will, if enacted in its current form, introduce a new power for the Charity Commission to exonerate the trustees of charities for breach of trust. See Appendix C, para C.6.

B.46   The concerns of consultees might suggest that an open-ended default power of the sort set out in the CP would be positively harmful in the non-charitable trust context. The general availability of the power would allow trustees to charge the cost of premiums to the trust fund, no matter how high (either in absolute terms or in proportion to the value of the trust). Whereas excessive insurance premiums would be likely to be apparent in advance of the appointment of a trustee where the cost of insurance is passed on in fees, a default power of the type proposed would allow previously unspecified costs to be incurred after the establishment of the trust. The difficulties could be even greater in relation to illiquid trusts as trustees would have to be able to sell trust assets to meet the costs of insurance.

B.47   It would be possible to make the availability of the general power subject to express contrary intention in the trust instrument. However, we consider that there is a real danger that the majority of settlors would fail to recognise the existence or importance of the default power and so would fail to exclude the power, no matter how inappropriate it would be. Even if settlors were appraised of the matter, the volatility of the insurance market would make it difficult for them to assess the ongoing cost of insurance at the time of disposition.

B.48   It would also be possible to provide a limited power subject to safeguards of the sort suggested in the Charities Bill.[16] However, we see difficulties with an extension of the power in the Charities Bill to non-charitable trusts. Outside the charitable sphere it is more difficult to assess objectively whether the purchase of insurance is in the best interests of the trust and whether appropriate care has been taken in making the decision. For example, where trustees have the means to be able to meet most claims for breach of trust personally, beneficiaries would not obtain any financial benefit from the trustees being insured. Permitting trustee indemnity insurance to be purchased might make it easier to obtain skilled trustees, or to obtain them for less cost, but this would in many cases be difficult to establish. Such benefits would have to be in some way balanced against the cost of insuring those particular trustees.

B.49   Assessing what it in the best interests of private beneficiaries would not, therefore, be straightforward. As the validity of the exercise of the power would depend on such an assessment and would be capable of being challenged by an individual beneficiary it could lead to uncertainty and litigation.

B.50   There are also policy reasons why the power proposed in the Charities Bill may be considered only necessary or appropriate in the charitable context. There is a strong public interest in encouraging individuals to act as trustees of charitable trusts. Allowing the trustees to insure can provide some such encouragement by giving them a degree of comfort that they will not be exposed to personal liability.

B.51   The Charity Commission currently receives many applications under section 26 of the Charities Act 1993 for authorisation to purchase indemnity insurance out of

---

[16]   Indeed, any power would be subject to the fundamental safeguard that it would have to be exercised in the best interests of the beneficiaries.

the charity's funds.[17] That so many of these applications are granted indicates that the Charity Commission believes the power for charitable trustees to purchase indemnity insurance to be in the public interest. The default power contained in the Charities Bill can therefore be seen simply as a logical extension of the current position, avoiding the need for so many routine applications to the Charity Commission.

Rejection of a default power

B.52   We are unconvinced that in the light of the recommendations of this paper and other developments there remains a pressing need for a statutory power of trustee indemnity insurance. The Charities Bill will introduce a default power for charitable trusts. Paid trustees will continue to be able to pass on the cost of insurance via their fees. Settlors will, where they consider it appropriate, continue to be able to authorise payments of indemnity insurance premiums out of the trust fund by express provision.

B.53   Furthermore, we are unable to disentangle the CP's provisional proposal in favour of a power to fund trustee indemnity insurance from its proposal to restrict trustee reliance on exemption clauses. The question of whether trustees should have a default power to purchase insurance out of the trust fund, otherwise than as a means of overcoming the perceived problems with exemption clauses, is outside the terms of reference of this project.[18]

B.54   We have therefore decided not to confirm our provisional proposal regarding trustee indemnity insurance. We believe the current position should continue. A trustee of a non-charitable trust will only have power to fund indemnity insurance from a trust if expressly authorised to do so by the trust instrument.

---

[17]   Charities 1993, s 26(1): "Subject to the provisions of this section, where it appears to the Commissioners that any action proposed or contemplated in the administration of a charity is expedient in the interests of the charity, they may by order sanction that action, whether or not it would otherwise be within the powers exercisable by the charity trustees in the administration of the charity; and anything done under the authority of such an order shall be deemed to be properly done in the exercise of those powers".

[18]   See CP, para 1.11.

APPENDIX C
CHARITABLE TRUSTS, PENSION TRUSTS AND COMMERCIAL TRUSTS

C.1   During the course of consultation many argued that regulation (of the sort provisionally proposed in the CP or otherwise) was not appropriate for specific types of trust. This Appendix considers in some detail the arguments made for the different treatment of charitable trusts, pension trusts and commercial trusts.

C.2   Many argued that the English law trust has now expanded beyond its original private sphere, and that the same policy considerations do not apply to the wide range of trusts that are now encountered. Consultation responses discussed four broad categories of trust: family trusts, charitable trusts, pension trusts and commercial trusts. Many felt that regulation of the sort envisaged by the CP should be restricted to family trusts. Charitable trusts and pension trusts are already subject to extensive legislative regulation, and, they contended, there is no strong case for this to be extended. Commercial trusts may or may not be subject to legislative regulation, but the overwhelming view was that market forces should be allowed to prevail.

C.3   Many consultees were of the impression that the Commission had formulated its provisional policy with the operation of the traditional family trust in mind. It is, of course, fair to say that almost all the reported cases in which trustee exemption clauses have been challenged have concerned "private" trusts of this kind.

C.4   It should be born in mind that consultees' comments about the place of exemption provisions in such trusts must be read against a backdrop of the type of legislative regulation provisionally proposed by the CP. Our revised non-statutory approach to regulation provides a significantly different context. However, many of the arguments hold good and have influenced our recommendations on the scope and application of the rule to different types of trust.[1]

CHARITABLE TRUSTS

C.5   The CP did not make any specific proposals for the regulation of charity trustees. The implication was therefore that the proposed general regulation of liability exemption and duty modification clauses should apply equally to the trustees of charitable and non-charitable trusts.

---

[1]   As set out in our guidance to the rule of practice: see para 6.80 and following.

C.6 Following the CP, the Government published its long-awaited draft Charities Bill.[2] This is of relevance in this context in two respects. First, it gives the Charity Commission power to exonerate the trustees of charities for breaches of trust, equivalent to the discretion given to the court under section 61 of the Trustee Act 1925.[3] Such a provision would clearly have some impact on the personal liability of charity trustees. Secondly, it grants charity trustees a default power to fund the purchase of indemnity insurance from the trust. This power is discussed in detail in Appendix B.[4]

C.7 Three specific issues emerged from consultation about the application of the CP's provisionally proposed scheme to charities.

C.8 The greatest concern was with the importance of framing regulation in such a way that would not discourage unpaid professionals from accepting gratuitous trusteeship of charitable trusts. We have already taken account of these concerns in re-formulating our distinction between different categories of trustee. This matches the suggestion of many consultees involved in the charity sector and we hope alleviates the majority of their concerns.

C.9 The second concern related to the technical possibility that the Charity Commission could refuse registration to a trust which has wide exemption clauses in its trust instrument on the basis that the trust's purposes are not exclusively charitable. The Charity Law Association noted that "while…the Charity Commission generally permits inclusion of fairly broad trustee exemption clauses in trust deeds at the point of registration, there is a lack of clarity as to the Charity Commission's overall attitude to these clauses and as to whether charity trustees can in fact rely upon these clauses with any degree of certainty".

C.10 We do not comment on the Charity Commission's interpretation of the potential effect of trustee exemption clauses on charitable status. We have, however, made the Charity Commission aware of the comments made in consultation.

C.11 The final issue was whether some attempt should be made to harmonise the position of charitable trusts and charitable companies. The Charity Law Association took issue with the CP's comments about the difference between the two forms of charity. It argued that "the key point in practice is the Charity Commission's attitude to trustee exemption, which applies to all charities whether they are trustees of incorporated charities or not…it would not be true to state that there is any substantial inequality between trusts and charitable companies." Whether or not this is the case, we do not consider harmonisation to be within the scope of this project.

[2] Based on Cabinet Office Strategy Unit, *Private Action, Public Benefit: A Review of Charities and the Wider Not-For-Profit Sector* (September 2002). The draft Bill was published by the Home Office on 27 May 2004. It was subject to pre-legislative scrutiny by the House of Lords and House of Commons Joint Committee on the Draft Charities Bill, which published a Report on 30 September 2004: HL Paper 167-I, HC 660-I. The Government published its Response to the Joint Committee's report on 21 December 2004 (Cm 6440) and published the Charities Bill. The Bill was introduced in the House of Lords on 20 December 2004, where it remains under consideration.

[3] See Charities Bill, cl 38, entitled "Power of Commission to relieve trustees, auditors etc. from liability for breach of trust or duty".

[4] Appendix B, para B.39 and following.

C.12 More generally, consultees put forward a number of arguments supporting the view that the use of trustee exemption clauses by charity trustees should be subject to a high level of control. Charitable trusts operate for the benefit of the public and so there are no specific beneficiaries able to take action against the trustees. They have access to special forms of tax relief and other forms of public funding. The trustees of charities are more likely to be successful in any attempt to escape liability, as the courts generally treat them more leniently than ordinary trustees.

C.13 On the other hand, there are good policy reasons why charity trustees should be able to protect themselves using exemption clauses. It is clearly in the public interest that charities should be able to continue to attract volunteers to act as trustees (in the same way as they are able to attract volunteers to carry out other tasks). Any tightening in the control of charity trustees could have undesirable consequences as the fear of liability could discourage potential trustees from accepting trusteeship. No matter how altruistic the individual, the possibility of personal financial liability is a strong disincentive to action.

C.14 Our conclusions on the application of our revised recommendations for regulation are set out at paragraph 6.86 and following. For the reasons given, the rule of practice can only properly be applied in relation to the original settlor, who is involved in establishing the terms of the trust. However, we have also held discussions with the Charity Commission who are considering the scope for increasing donor awareness by issuing advice on the subject of trustee exemption clauses.

C.15 The main form of liability protection for charity trustees will remain liability insurance. The Charities Bill default power will facilitate this.

PENSION TRUSTS

C.16 The CP did not give specific consideration to pension trusts. The implication was that the trustees of pension trusts would be subject to any regulation of trustee exemption clauses.

C.17 A number of consultees considered that the Law Commission had failed adequately to take account of the different considerations which apply to pension trusts. Many questioned whether regulation of trustee exemption clauses should apply to the pensions industry, which utilises the trust structure but only as part of an established system subject to its own close regulation.

Arguments against regulation

C.18 Several differences between pension trusts and other types of trust were put forward as arguments against the regulation of pension trustees.

Pension trusts already subject to considerable regulation

C.19   The duties of pension trustees are already supplemented by obligations and requirements imposed by the Pensions Act 1995. Trustee exclusion is already regulated under section 33(1).[5]

C.20   This provision may not be as significant an incursion into the pension trustee's freedom to exclude liability as it first appears: the evidence which emerged from consultation is that in practice the investment decisions of almost all pension schemes are delegated to experienced fund managers.[6] However, the fact that it was decided to limit restriction to this relatively limited extent may suggest that more extensive regulation is inappropriate.

C.21   Consultees also pointed out that, as well as their own regulatory structure, pension schemes have their own regulator, the Occupational Pensions Regulatory Authority ("OPRA"), which can impose sanctions on trustees such as penalties and prohibition orders. Under the Pensions Act 2004, OPRA was replaced by the Pensions Regulator[7] with a brief to protect the benefits of members of occupational pension schemes and new sanctions against employers and trustees.

C.22   Beneficiaries under occupational pension schemes, in addition to their common law remedies, may complain to the Pensions Ombudsman that they have been the victims of maladministration. This extends beyond breach of trust law and statutory duties, and can encompass acts that are clearly within the standards set out in specific legislation.

Trend to reduce the regulatory burdens on pension trustees

C.23   Consultees drew attention to Government initiatives to lighten regulation and assist the continuation of existing employer sponsored schemes and the encouragement of new schemes. This reflects the sentiment of the Pickering Report which said that:

> This simple concept [the pension] has been made extremely complicated. This complication does not simply add unnecessary costs...it acts as a disincentive to pension accumulation. Consumers are put off, employers are discouraged and those commercial providers whose products might otherwise help finance a secure old age are extremely frustrated as their pursuit of cost-effective products is hampered by intrusive and often ill-focused regulation.[8]

The prevalence of employee trustees in pension schemes

C.24   Many consultees pointed to the importance of member-nominated trustees in pension trusts. Over-regulation of trustee exemption clauses could deter many

---

[5] See para 2.32.

[6] The scheme trustees are consequently not liable in any case for negligent investment decisions, unless they were themselves negligent in the selection of their delegate.

[7] The Pensions Act received Royal Assent on 18 November 2004. The Pensions Regulator replaced OPRA on 6 April 2005.

[8] A Pickering, *A Simpler Way to Better Pensions* (2002).

lay trustees from assuming responsibility in the first place. The Pensions Act 2004 requires one third of pension trustees to be nominated by scheme members.[9] The Myners Review[10] recommended that member trustees of pension trusts should receive payment in order to encourage them to take on trusteeships, notwithstanding that they do not have special expertise or experience.

C.25 A critical element of the possible forms of regulation discussed in the CP and recommended in this Report is the distinction between paid trustees and those that act gratuitously. This distinction causes problems where there is acceptance that trustees who are in every other sense "lay" may receive payment for accepting the role.

Arguments in favour of regulation

C.26 There are also strong arguments to support the view that there is a particular need for the regulation of reliance on trustee exemption clauses by pension trustees.

Employment relationship

C.27 Responding to the CP, the Pensions Ombudsman commented that "beneficiaries of [a pension] trust, ie the employees who are members of the pension scheme, would see themselves as being in a very different situation than the beneficiaries of a family trust. They would see the pension scheme as part of their employment relationship". A clause exempting liability for negligence would appear to have little place in such a relationship.

C.28 An argument was put forward that this relationship should mitigate against regulation. It was suggested that the ongoing funding liability of the employer towards the scheme means that it is the employers rather than the beneficiaries that will suffer the effects of any loss which the scheme cannot recover. This argument only goes so far. Where employers are insolvent there will be no further source of funds to make good any loss caused to the trust fund by the actions or omissions of trustees protected by exemption provisions.

Provision of consideration by beneficiaries

C.29 The beneficiaries of pension trusts provide consideration for their benefits. This may take the form of monetary contributions by the scheme member or, in the case of occupational pensions, service. A number of consultees suggested that pension trustees should consequently be subject to more stringent regulation than other trustees.

Proper protection of pensioners

C.30 Whatever the technical differences between pension trusts and other trusts, there are policy grounds for stronger protection of pension trust funds because of the important role those funds play. Although vulnerable individuals may be dependant on other sorts of trust fund, it is almost invariably the case that

---

[9] Pensions Act 2004, s 241.

[10] P Myners, *Institutional Investment in the United Kingdom: A Review* (2001).

members of a pension scheme will to a greater or lesser extent rely on their pension in their retirement. Trustee exemption clauses have the capacity to protect trustees from liability to make good losses caused to the pension fund. Pensioners may consequently be left without pensions.

Conclusion

C.31   We accept as a matter of principle the view that pension trusts should be considered a separate category of trust and so be excluded from our proposed regulation of trustee exemption clauses.[11] This matches the general trend of taking the law governing pension trusts away from general trust law[12] and supports the view that pension trusts should be governed by rules specific to their needs.

C.32   As we discuss in Part 6,[13] it would, in any case, be difficult to apply our recommended rule of practice to all pension schemes. In occupational pension schemes the employer acts as primary settlor.[14] The settlor will be a market equal of the trustee and almost certainly legally advised. There is therefore little point in drawing the employer's attention to trustee exemption provisions. The members of the pension scheme can also be seen to be settlors to the extent of their contributions[15] in addition to their position as beneficiaries. The rule could apply so as to require their attention to be drawn to exemption provisions in the scheme document. However, this would be of little practical purpose: employees are not generally presented with a choice of occupational pension and so are unable to choose a trust without an exemption clause. They must take what they are offered.

COMMERCIAL TRUSTS

C.33   Many consultees argued that the objectives of the Law Commission in this project are not relevant to commercial trusts and their trustees.

C.34   A number of the arguments made by consultees against the application of the CP's proposed regulation to commercial trusts have been discussed in previous parts of this paper with reference to trusts generally:

   (1)   The effectiveness and viability of commercial trusts rests on all the parties being certain as to their respective rights, powers and obligations.

---

[11]   It has been argued that pension trusts are a *sui generis* species of trust and operate on different principles from traditional trusts: David Hayton, "Pension trusts and traditional trusts: drastically different species of trusts" [2005] *Conveyancer and Property Lawyer* 229.

[12]   Reflected in provisions of the Trustee Act 2000 which excludes the application of several parts of that Act to occupational pension schemes.

[13]   See para 6.84.

[14]   See *Hayton and Marshall, Commentary and Cases on the Law of Trusts and Equitable Remedies* (11th ed 2001) at p 737.

[15]   "While the employer in setting up the pension trust with a nominal amount of money is a settlor, it is now clear that when an employee joins the scheme and makes his or her first contribution he or she becomes settlor of his or her settlement": *Hayton and Marshall, Commentary and Cases on the Law of Trusts and Equitable Remedies* (11th ed 2001) p 737. See also *Air Jamaica Ltd v Charlton* [1999] 1 WLR 1399.

(2)   If regulation caused the validity of the "passive functions" of commercial trustees to become uncertain they would be required to monitor the trust funds actively, placing additional burdens upon trustees and generating additional costs.

(3)   If trustee exemption clauses, duty modification clauses and extended powers clauses are regulated, the trustees of commercial trusts would become more reluctant to exercise their discretionary powers.

(4)   Indemnity insurance for commercial trustees is either prohibitively expensive or unavailable, as the market does not have the capacity to insure commercial trustees.

(5)   Commercial trustees generally do not invoke exemption clauses to escape liability because of the negative impact upon their market reputation that would ensue.

C.35   We have commented on the strengths and weaknesses of these arguments in the contexts in which they were first raised. The following points specific to commercial trusts also emerged from consultation.

Commercial trusts are negotiated by market equals

C.36   The Association of Corporate Trustees and the International Paying Agents Association gave the example of a company issuing bonds. The terms of the bonds will typically have been negotiated by an investment bank and will be fully described in an offering document which must be made available to potential investors. The investors are sophisticated market professionals or institutions who are fully aware of the investment risk attached to any issue and the powers and duties (and the limitations of those powers and duties) of a trustee appointed by the issuer to represent their interests.

Many commercial trusts arise out of contract rather than by way of gift

C.37   The Financial Markets Law Committee Report ("FMLC Report") points out that, in contrast with family trusts, "the commercial trust arises out of contract rather than the traditional transfer of property by way of gift".[16] Consequently, the Report argues, the trustee/beneficiary relationship in such arrangements is in many ways closer in substance to contracts between sophisticated parties with the freedom to contract, than to a traditional trust relationship.

C.38   This argument can only be taken so far, as obviously the relationship is more than a contractual one (else the market would feel no need to make use of trusts at all). However, it does highlight the different dynamics of commercial trusts.

Commercial trustees rely on trustee exemption clauses to protect them from the aggressive tactics of "vulture fund" investors

C.39   A number of consultees raised the problem of "vulture fund" investors. Such investors purchase distressed issues for an amount lower than their face value in

---

[16] Financial Markets Law Committee, *Trustee Exemption Clauses Report – Issue 62* (May 2004) p 1.

the hope that by rejecting otherwise sensible compromises they will be paid out in a short time frame at a price which will give them a good return on their investment.

C.40   Trustee exemption clauses are crucial if a trustee faced by such aggressive beneficiaries is to be able to operate in the interests of the beneficiaries as a whole without giving rise to the prospect of a legal challenge. Exemption clauses have the practical effect of preventing speculative breach of trust claims arising. If a claim is made it can be robustly defended and an application made to strike it out.[17] The trustees can therefore avoid the full expense and resource implications of defending the claim.

The damaging consequences of excessive regulation

C.41   The FMLC Report claims that if the Law Commission's provisional proposals were implemented "there is likely to be an extremely detrimental effect on the international markets in London".[18]

C.42   The Report suggests that "restrictions on the power of a trustee to exclude liability may mean that the trust structure is discarded altogether in favour of other structures. In the context of the capital markets, for example, the alternative would be a fiscal agency."[19] This, the Report suggests, would not be in the interests of the market, as the fiscal agency system is less flexible than the use of a trust and less in keeping with the market's "general move towards collective action".[20] It would not be in the national interest as it would be "damaging not only to the corporate sector in general, but also to London's position as an international centre for corporate finance".[21]

C.43   The FMLC Report points out that much of London's financial business is international, and that it is only because English law is considered to be favourable that such law is adopted. If the certainty that arrangements governed by English law currently enjoys is undermined, English law "could easily be discarded" and "in the longer term, it is likely that the considerable areas of financial business currently based in London and dependent on traditional English trust law may move their operations to less restrictive jurisdictions".[22]

---

[17]   See Civil Procedure Rules, r 3.4.

[18]   Financial Markets Law Committee, *Trustee Exemption Clauses Report – Issue 62* (May 2004) p 2.

[19]   Financial Markets Law Committee, *Trustee Exemption Clauses Report – Issue 62* (May 2004) p 2.

[20]   As recommended in the *Report of the G-10 Working Group on Contractual Clauses* (September 2002).

[21]   Financial Markets Law Committee, *Trustee Exemption Clauses Report – Issue 62* (May 2004) p 2.

[22]   Financial Markets Law Committee, *Trustee Exemption Clauses Report – Issue 62* (May 2004) pp 2-3.

Many commercial trustees are already subject to extensive regulation

C.44   A number of specific statutory provisions regulate certain sorts of commercial trust. Part 2 has set out provisions regulating reliance on exemption clauses in unit trusts and debenture trusts.[23]

Conclusion

C.45   We accept that there are a number of very good reasons why the use of trustee exemption clauses does not need to be regulated in some commercial trust situations. The arguments for and against regulation made by consultees are, in this area perhaps more than any other, dependant on the type of regulation in question. We comment on the application of our proposed rule of practice to commercial trusts in Part 6.[24]

---

[23]   Respectively, Financial Services and Markets Act 2000 s 253; Companies Act 1985, s 192; and Pensions Act 1995, s 33. See paras 2.27 to 2.32.

[24]   See guidance to the rule of practice, para 6.80 and following.

APPENDIX D
DISTINGUISHING BETWEEN DIFFERENT SORTS OF DUTY MODIFICATION

TYPES OF CLAUSE

D.1 Duty modification provisions can operate in a number of different ways. We see three main categories of use.

Type 1: trustee not permitted to act

D.2 This type of clause restricts the trustee's powers in the relevant area of operation and therefore prevents the trustee from acting in a certain way. For example, "the trustee shall not interfere in the management or conduct of the business of any company whose shares, stocks, securities, debentures, debenture stock or loan capital are comprised in the trust fund". Such clauses allow the demarcation of the respective roles of the trustee and others.

D.3 The clause explicitly takes away any power the trustee would otherwise have to do what the clause prohibits.

Type 2: trustee not bound to act

D.4 This type of clause (which we believe to be the most common formulation) removes or modifies the strict duty of the trustee to do or not to do a particular thing. For example, "the trustee shall not be under a duty to interfere in the management or conduct of the business of any company whose shares, stocks, securities, debentures, debenture stock or loan capital are comprised in the trust fund".

D.5 The clause does not explicitly limit the trustee's powers.

Type 3: trustee permitted to act and not liable for failure to act

D.6 This type of clause combines duty modification with exclusion of liability. For example, "the trustee shall not be under a duty to interfere in the management or conduct of the business of any company whose shares, stocks, securities, debentures, debenture stock or loan capital are comprised in the trust fund and shall not be liable for any failure to do so".

D.7 The first part of the clause modifies the trustee's strict duty to interfere. The clause does not explicitly limit the trustee's powers.

D.8 The second part excuses the trustee from any liability that might result from failing to exercise its power to interfere.

EFFECT OF THE THREE TYPES OF CLAUSE ON LIABILITY FOR NEGLIGENCE

Type 1: trustee not permitted to act

D.9 A type 1 clause prohibits the trustee from acting. It would constitute a breach of trust for the trustee to act in the way prohibited by the clause. The trustee cannot be considered to be negligent in failing to act in breach of trust and the clause therefore does not have the effect of permitting the trustee to act negligently.

Type 3: trustee permitted to act and not liable for failure to act

D.10   It is equally clear that a type 3 clause which combines modification of the trustee's duty with exclusion of liability does permit trustee negligence in circumstances where the trustee negligently fails to act. Any liability arising from such negligence is excluded.

Type 2: trustee not bound to act

D.11   The effect of a type 2 clause is more difficult. The clause clearly removes the strict liability that would otherwise flow from the breach of the trustee's duty to act. However, it does not expressly restrict the trustee's powers and does not expressly exclude liability. There is no clear authority as to whether the clause permits negligence. As the following paragraphs demonstrate, whether or not the clause permits negligence depends on how it is construed.

Trustee liable for negligent exercise or non-exercise of the power

D.12   One possible interpretation focuses on the fact that type 2 clauses do not expressly modify the trustee's powers. It is therefore strongly arguable that such clauses have no effect on those powers or the potential liability attaching to them. If this is the case, and the trustee remains free to act or not to act according to its discretion, liability may still flow from the negligent exercise or non-exercise of the powers. On this construction a type 2 duty modification clause does not protect a trustee who acts negligently or negligently fails to act.

D.13   Take the example of a clause providing that a trustee is not obliged to interfere in the management or conduct of the business of any company whose shares are comprised in the trust fund. Even if the effect of the clause is to allow the trustee not to take certain steps necessary to fulfil the wider trustee duty to safeguard trust assets properly, the clause simply provides an authorisation not to act. As the trustee retains the power to act, any failure to exercise that power properly may still result in liability. This would include failing to act when the trustee ought properly to act, as well as acting improperly. The duty modification clause does not authorise negligence: it merely takes away strict liability.

D.14   This view finds support in *Hayton and Marshall*:

> It needs also to be noted that even if a clause ousts the trustee's duty as controlling shareholder of a company to seek information on the company's activities and to monitor such activities unless having actual knowledge of dishonesty in the running of the company, the trustee by virtue of its controlling shareholding has *power* to intervene and so could still be liable for negligent failure to exercise this power in circumstances considered by the court to require the power to be exercised.[1]

---

[1]   *Hayton and Marshall, Commentary and Cases on the Law of Trusts and Equitable Remedies* (11th ed 2001) p 792.

Trustee not liable for negligent exercise or non-exercise of the power

D.15   An alternative interpretation is that the effect of a type 2 clause providing that the trustee shall not be under a duty to interfere is to exclude all obligations to interfere, howsoever arising. The clause removes the strict liability that would otherwise flow from the breach of the trustee's duty to interfere. Furthermore, the clause operates so as to preclude the trustee from being liable for any failure to exercise its power to interfere appropriately.

D.16   The logical basis for this construction is that the clause not only excludes the trustee's strict duty to interfere, it also takes away the trustee's duty to act in the best interests of the beneficiaries to the extent that so acting would comprise interfering. As there is no duty to act in the best interests of the beneficiaries in this context, there is no basis for liability if the trustee fails to interfere appropriately. Under this interpretation the clause would have the effect of authorising the trustee to act negligently.

D.17   However, we think that it is extremely unlikely that a court would adopt this interpretation. If it did, it is possible that the provision would be invalidated in the light of *Armitage v Nurse*,[2] which appears to treat the duty to act in the beneficiaries' best interests as a core duty of trusteeship which cannot be excluded.

Our preferred view

D.18   We prefer the interpretation that type 2 duty modification clauses address only the implied duty to do a particular thing and do not affect the underlying powers to act. This position accords with the basic principles of trust law and is, to some extent, acknowledged by the widespread use of simple duty modification clauses supported by liability exclusion clauses.[3]

D.19   However, the point is unclear. It might, on the facts, be appropriate to take an entirely different approach; for example, construing the provision as a type 3 clause, impliedly excluding liability for negligence. It is likely that a court faced with the task of analysing such a clause would have regard to factors such as evidence of the intention of the parties, the other terms of the trust, the previous actions of the trustee and whether the duty from which the trustee is excused is imposed on a third party.

CONSTRUING PARTICULAR DUTY MODIFICATION PROVISIONS

D.20   The analysis above attempts to establish the effect of three types of duty modification clause. However, in practice duty modification clauses often do not precisely follow one of these forms. Where a clause is of itself difficult to decipher, it cannot easily be assigned to one of the three types, and consequently its technical operation may be even less clear.

D.21   The difficulties of construing a given clause can be seen by reference to the example of a provision that "it is not the trustee's responsibility to interfere in the

---

[2]   [1998] Ch 241.

[3]   See para 5.86. If simple duty modification clauses are themselves protective, what is the need for associated liability exclusion?

management or conduct of the business of any company whose shares are comprised in the trust fund". We see a number of possible constructions of "not the trustee's responsibility":

(1) trustee not permitted to act;

(2) trustee not under strict duty to act, but retains power to act and liable for negligent exercise or non-exercise of power;

(3) trustee retains power to act, but under no duty to act in the beneficiaries' best interests and so no basis for liability for negligent exercise or non-exercise of power; or

(4) trustee permitted to act and not liable for failure to act.

D.22 The construction of duty modification clauses worded in this type of manner is therefore particularly difficult. It is unlikely that an adviser would be able to be confident of the correct construction of such clauses if asked to advise. A conclusive interpretation is likely only to be available on application to a court, taking into account the factors referred to in paragraph D.19.

CONCLUSION

D.23 We believe that the correct construction of a clearly worded duty modification clause, which does not expressly restrict the trustees' powers and does not expressly exclude liability, is that it does not have the effect of protecting the trustee from liability for negligence. However, we accept that the opposite interpretation can also be argued. There is no authority to support either view.

D.24 Clauses such as "it is not the trustee's responsibility" to do a certain thing, are susceptible to a number of possible interpretations.

APPENDIX E
PUBLICLY RECORDED TRUST INFORMATION

E.1 Since publication of the CP the Commission has attempted to gather statistics about trusts from the Inland Revenue, the Charity Commission and the Probate Registry. The figures that we have obtained are set out below.

E.2 However, none of these organisations are able to provide comprehensive figures:

(1) Trustees only have to notify HM Revenue and Customs when they become liable to pay tax, and many of them do not actually have taxable income or gains in any given year. The Revenue figures do not take account of, for example, life assurance policies held in trust.

(2) The Charity Commission has provided us with approximate figures for the number of charities on its register, but it is impossible to know in how many of these charities the property is held on trust.[1] There are also an indeterminate number of charities which are not registered because they are small, or are otherwise excepted or exempted from registration.

(3) The London Probate Registry compiles statistics relating to grants of representation but do not record the number of wills that contain trusts.

INFORMATION PROVIDED BY THE CHARITY COMMISSION

E.3 As at 31 March 2006, there were 167,202 "main" charities on the register, and approximately 13,000 "subsidiary" charities co-registered with main charities because of links between them.[2] In most of these cases the property will be held on trust, the major exceptions to this being charitable companies and charitable industrial and provident societies, of which there are estimated to be 10,000 in all.

E.4 There is, however, an indeterminate number of other charities (estimated at 50,000) which are not registered because they are small, or otherwise excepted or exempted from registration. It is impossible to know in how many of these cases the property is held on trust.

---

[1] See Appendix C for the alternative ways in which charities may be constituted.

[2] Information provided by the Charity Commission. See Charity Commission, *Quarterly Facts & Figures and Tables for 2006 – 1st Quarter* (2006), available at http://www.charitycommission.gov.uk/registeredcharities/factfigures.asp (last visited 16 June 2006).

INFORMATION PROVIDED BY HM CUSTOMS AND REVENUE

Table 1: number of trusts in the Self Assessment system

Tax Year Ending	Live Taxpayers (000s)
2001	341
2002	343
2003	345
2004	342
2005	333

Table 2: number of returns issued and filed (including nil returns)

Tax Year Ending	Returns Issued (000s)	Returns Filed (000s)	Data Updated
2001	298	297	14 April 05
2002	299	297	14 April 05
2003	290	285	3 April 05
2004	277	266	12 June 05
2005	224	36	12 June 05

Table 3: number of returns showing a tax charge processed

Tax Year Ending	Number of Returns (000s)	Bare Trusts (000s)	Discretionary Trusts (000s)
1997	235	9	77
1998	243	5	86
1999	224	3	90
2000	221	2	94
2001	221	2	97
2002	226	2	100
2003	222	2	106
2004	213	2	107

APPENDIX F
ORGANISATIONS CONSULTED ON THE RULE
OF PRACTICE

Association of Contentious Trust and Probate Specialists

Association of Corporate Trustees

British Bankers' Association

Charity Commission

Financial Services Authority

HM Treasury

Institute of Chartered Accountants in England and Wales

Institute of Professional Willwriters

Law Society (Wills and Equity Committee)

Pensions Ombudsman

Society of Trust and Estate Practitioners

Society of Will Writers

Trust Law Committee

APPENDIX G
RULE OF PRACTICE ADOPTED BY THE SOCIETY OF TRUST AND ESTATE PRACTITIONERS

The England and Wales Committee of the Society of Trust and Estate Practitioners has approved the following rule which will in due course be annexed to the STEP Code, together with guidance notes on its detailed application.

STEP RULE

(1)   Where a member prepares, or causes to be prepared, a will or other testamentary document or a trust instrument (each an **"Instrument"**), or is aware of being named as an original trustee or executor in an Instrument:

      (i)   in which he, or any trustee or executor, is entitled to remuneration under the terms of the Instrument; or

      (ii)   where he has, or may expect to have, a Financial Interest in the trusteeship or executorship of the trust or will or the preparation of the Instrument; and

    (b)   any one or more of the circumstances described in paragraph 2 below applies (together **"the Disclosable Circumstances"**),

such member shall use his reasonable endeavours to ensure:

      (i)   that he or another shall have notified the Settlor of the provisions in the Instrument or the original trustee or executor's terms and conditions relating to the Disclosable Circumstances; and

      (ii)   that he has reasonable grounds for believing that the Settlor has given his full and informed acceptance of such provisions prior to his execution or approval of the Instrument.

(2)   The Disclosable Circumstances referred to in paragraph 1 above are the existence of provisions in the Instrument or the original trustee or executor's terms and conditions the effect of which limit or exclude the liability of a trustee or executor for negligence.

(3)   In this rule

    (a)   **"Financial Interest"** means circumstances where the member benefits or reasonably expects to benefit (whether directly or indirectly) from providing a service as trust advisor or as trustee.

(b) **"Settlor"** means any person who would be a principal initial settlor in relation to a settlement, or at whose directions the Instrument is created.

(4) This rule shall be subordinate to any legislation or other binding provision of law in any jurisdiction where the member shall practice and shall only apply to Instruments governed by the law of England and Wales.

APPENDIX H
RESPONDENTS TO CONSULTATION PAPER NO 171

RESPONDENTS TO CONSULTATION PAPER NO 171

Mr Trevor Aldridge QC

Allen and Overy

Association of Charitable Foundations

Association of Contentious Trust and Probate Specialists

Association of Corporate Treasurers

Association of Corporate Trustees and International Paying Agents Association

Association of District Judges

Association of Pension Lawyers

Association of Private Client Investment Managers and Stockbrokers

Attorney General and Solicitor General

Bar Council Law Reform Committee

Barclays Bank Trust Company Ltd

His Honour Judge Behrens

Bristol Law Society Trust, Tax and Probate Sub-Committee

British Association for Counselling and Psychotherapy

British Bankers' Association Estates and Trusts Committee

Cancer Research UK

Capita IRG Trustees Ltd

Ms Janette Cattell, Mr Christopher Groves, Ms Jane Holmes, Ms Judith Ingham, Ms Justine Markovitz, Ms Samantha Morgan and Ms Katharine West, solicitors

Ms Esther Cavett and Ms Johanna Pass, Clifford Chance

Chancery Bar Association

Charity Commission

Charity Law Association

Citicorp Trustee Company Ltd

City of Westminster and Holborn Law Society

Clifford Chance

Mr Jonathan Cooke, Humphrey & Co

CRESTCo Ltd

Mr Derek Davies, Emeritus Fellow at St Catherine's College, University of Oxford

Mr John Davies, solicitor

Mr Howard Dellar, Lee Bolton & Lee Solicitors

Denton Wilde Sapte

Department for Work and Pensions

Depositary and Trustee Association

Deutsche Trustee Company Ltd

Mr Stephen Edell

Eversheds

Freshfields Bruckhaus Deringer (Employment, Pensions and Benefits Department)

Freshfields Bruckhaus Deringer (Structured Finance Team)

Mr Simon Gardner, University of Oxford

Dr Joshua Getzler, University of Oxford

Mr Andrew Goldstone, solicitor

Mr Charles Gothard, solicitor

Halliwell Landau

Hammonds Pensions Disputes Team

Mr Mark Herbert, barrister

Herbert Smith

High Court Judges of the Chancery Division

Mr Gregory Hill, barrister

Mr Alan Howells

Mr C I Howells, barrister

HSBC Bank Plc

HSBC Trust Company (UK) Ltd

Institute of Chartered Accountants in England and Wales

Institute of Chartered Secretaries and Administrators

Mr Richard Jackson, accountant

Mr Michael Jacobs, solicitor

Mr C M Jarman, Payne Hicks Beach

Ms Nicola Kemp, solicitor

Professor Ann Kenny, University of Northumbria

Professor Roger Kerridge, Mr Simon Baughen and Dr Stephen Watterson, University of Bristol

Mr Trevor Lake, Marie Curie Cancer Care

Mr David Laverick, Pensions Ombudsman

The Law Debenture Pension Trust Corporation Plc

The Law Debenture Trust Corporation Plc

The Law Debenture Trustee for Charities

Law Reform Advisory Committee for Northern Ireland

The Law Society

Mr W A Lee

Linklaters

Loan Market Association

Mr Keith Lock, Office of the Official Solicitor and Public Trustee

London Endowed Charities Forum

Mr David Long, solicitor

Lovells

Macfarlanes

Mr John Ross Martyn, barrister

Ms Sophie Mazzier, solicitor

Mercer HR Consulting Ltd

Ms Judith Morris, Bircham Dyson Bell

Mr Roger Morton

National Association of Pension Funds

National Council for Voluntary Organisations

National Society for the Prevention of Cruelty to Children

The National Trust

The Notaries Society

Mr Edward Nugee QC, barrister

Occupational Pensions Regulatory Authority

Professor James Penner, King's College, London

Pensions Management Institute

Mr Robin Phipps, Macmillan Cancer Relief

Private Wealth Group, Allen & Overy

Prudential Trustee Company Ltd

Ms Francesca Quint, barrister

Rathbone Investment Management Ltd

Mr Nigel Reid, solicitor

Richards Butler, solicitors

Mr Paul Saunders

Dr Roger Sexton, Nottingham Trent University

Mr Geoffrey Shindler, solicitor

Society of Pension Consultants

Society of Trust and Estate Practitioners Technical Committee

Mr P F Smith, University of Reading

State Street Trustees Ltd

Mr J R Stephenson

Professor Mark Thompson, University of Leicester

Trust Law Committee

Lord Walker of Gestingthorpe

Watson Wyatt

Mr Gary Watt, University of Warwick

Ms Esther White, solicitor

Mr Richard Williams, solicitor

Mr Richard Wilson, barrister

Wilsons

Master Winegarten, Chief Chancery Master

Mr Philip Wood

PUBLISHED ARTICLES ON CONSULTATION PAPER NO 171

C Gothard, "Watch out trustees! Trustee exemption clauses – Law Commission Consultation Paper" (2003) 9(9) *Trusts and Trustees* 24

G Hill, "The debate over trustee exemption clauses" (2003) 47 *Amicus Curiae* 24

C I Howells, "Trustee exemption clauses" (2003) *New Law Journal* 565

M Jacobs, "Trustee Exemption Clauses: Another view" (June 2003) *Trusts and Estates Law Journal* 8

S Mazzier, "A question of trust" (14 April 2003) *The Lawyer* 29

J Morris, "The Law Commission's Consultation Paper on Trustee Exemption Clauses" (2003) Issue 3 *Private Client Business* 188

E White, "Inside View - The use and abuse of trustee exemption clauses" (10 Feb 2003) *Pensions Week*

Printed in the UK by The Stationery Office Limited
on behalf of the Controller of Her Majesty's Stationery Office
ID 5390323 07/06
Printed on Paper containing 75% post consumer waste and 25% ECF pulp.